# Our Father's
# WORLD

# Our Father's
# WORLD

Mobilizing the Church to Care for Creation

Edward Brown

*Care of Creation, Inc.*

*http://www.careofcreation.org*

DOORLIGHT PUBLICATIONS, SOUTH HADLEY, MA

First published 2006 by Doorlight Publications, P.O. Box 718, South Hadley, MA 01075.

Library of Congress Control Number: 2006938985
ISBN 0-9778372-2-X

Typeset with LATEX in Palatino. Printed and bound in the United States by Lightning Source Inc. (US) 1246 Heil Quaker Blvd. La Vergne, TN USA 37086

Cover photography provided by Michaela Harkner.
Cover art by John Tetreault.

For further information contact Care of Creation at PO Box 44582, Madison, WI 53744.

For Susanna,

my

*Rafiq-i-Hayat*

*This is my Father's world,*
*And to my listening ears*
*All nature sings, and round me rings*
*The music of the spheres.*
*This is my Father's world:*
*I rest me in the thought*
*Of rocks and trees, of skies and seas;*
*His hand the wonders wrought.*

*This is my Father's world,*
*The birds their carols raise,*
*The morning light, the lily white,*
*Declare their maker's praise.*
*This is my Father's world:*
*He shines in all that's fair;*
*In the rustling grass I hear him pass;*
*He speaks to me everywhere.*

*This is my Father's world.*
*O let me ne'er forget*
*That though the wrong seems oft so strong,*
*God is the ruler yet.*
*This is my Father's world:*
*Why should my heart be sad?*
*The Lord is King; let the heavens ring!*
*God reigns; let the earth be glad!*

Maltbie D. Babcock, 1901

# Contents

# Prologue

## December, 2004

"Sometimes you just have to leap, and build your wings on the way down."

That was the heading I used on a letter to friends and family in April, 2005, explaining why my wife and I were, with a missionary couple in Kenya, forming a new evangelical, environmental missions organization. Recently unemployed, with three college age children and no money in the bank, it didn't seem like the most rational decision I had ever made.

It started with an email message—and I can picture the scene in my mind:

"How would you like to help us?" It is a modern version of what students of missions often refer to as "the Macedonian call." In Acts 16, the Apostle Paul and a group traveling with him were unsure of where God wanted them to go next in their mission of sharing the good news about Jesus Christ. Paul had a dream of a man from Macedonia, a Roman province across the Aegean Sea from northern Turkey, where the party was at the time. "Come over and help us" said the man.

In my case, it is December, 2004, and I am sitting at my computer, very much awake. But the appeal could have been lifted right out of the pages of the New Testament: A missionary in Kenya is saying, "We need to start a new missions organization. Why don't you help us?"

Craig Sorley grew up in East Africa. He loves God and Africa, and he has a passion for caring for God's world. I've known Craig for a couple of years, and I have followed his efforts to establish an "environmental missions" project near

Nairobi. He's been trying to hold back a massive environmental crisis that has seen large parts of his childhood homeland suffer devastation and destruction on an unbelievable scale.

My job with Au Sable Institute, a Christian environmental organization, is about to disappear due to restructuring. My wife and I have been wrestling with what our future would be. Unemployment at age 51 with three children ready to go to college is not a pleasant prospect, but starting a brand new organization that is evangelical and environmental is more like walking on water—it would take that much faith and more. But Craig's invitation is intriguing and even tempting. I agree with his premise that the Church of Jesus Christ is the key to environmental healing. "We want to transform people and the land they live on."

You would have to call me a reluctant environmentalist. In twenty-five plus years of Christian ministry, I have a wide range of experience. I have been, at one time or another, a pastor, a campus minister for international students, a missionary, a missions administrator, a Chief Operating Officer, and most recently a Country Director for a Christian development organization responding to the Pakistan earthquake of 2005. I would never have predicted that I would find myself starting an environmental mission organization!

However, Craig's proposal has triggered a deep response in me. I have spent the last five years working with Calvin DeWitt, founder of Au Sable Institute, patriarch of the modern evangelical environmental movement in North America, and professor of Envirionmental Studies at University of Wisconsin-Madison. Though my responsibilities were not directly related to the Au Sable science program, I had the privilege of working closely with faculty members and students from more than 60 Christian colleges around the country. I was able to meet and learn from Sir Ghillian Prance, an Au Sable board member and one of the foremost horticultural experts in the world and Sir John Houghton, then head of the Intergovernmental Panel on

Climate Change (IPCC), with whom we collaborated in organizing an international climate conference in Oxford England in the summer of 2005. Among the guests at that conference were the Rev. Jim Ball of the Evangelical Environmental Network, soon to become known across the US for his "What Would Jesus Drive?" campaign, and the Rev. Richard Cizik of the National Association of Evangelicals, who has since become one of the most outspoken evangelical proponents of environmental action in the US, particularly with regard to climate change. This was an eventful five years that transformed my perspective on God, his creation, and the importance and urgency of the environmental crisis facing the world today.

I was becoming convinced that the answer to the environmental crisis is not with scientists. Science has made tremendous progress since Earth Day 1970, a date that represents both a national awakening on this topic, and my own first exposure to it as a junior in high school. Scientists have shown us how serious our problems are and they have come up with solutions. I have been surprised by the cautious optimism expressed by some prominent voices—believers and skeptics— that it is possible for the human race to navigate through the worst of the crisis in the next fifty or seventy five years. Scientists can only do so much, however. The future of God's creation—and the human race—is in the hands of politicians, businessmen and women, and lawyers. More than anyone else, creation is in the hands of present and future pastors, teachers and ordinary Christians. By the end of my tenure at Au Sable Institute, I had begun to believe that the Church of Jesus Christ, and the ordinary people who are its members, are the best and perhaps the only hope for a true solution to the global environmental crisis.

That sounds like an audacious claim. But now even secular voices are appealing to faith communities for help: In his recent book, *The Creation*, Harvard biologist and confirmed skeptic E. O. Wilson writes this appeal to a fictional Southern Baptist Pastor:

*You and I and every other human being strive for the*
*same imperatives of security, freedom of choice, personal*
*dignity, and a cause to believe in that is larger than our-*
*selves. Let us see, then, if we can, and you are willing, to*
*meet on the near side of metaphysics in order to deal with*
*the real world we share.* ***I put it this way because you***
***have the power to help solve a great problem about***
***which I care deeply.*** *I hope you have the same con-*
*cern. I suggest that we set aside our differences in order*
*to save the Creation...* ***Pastor, we need your help.*** *The*
*Creation—living Nature—is in deep trouble.* [Wilson
2006, 4; emphasis mine]

Wilson could have phrased his appeal a bit more tactfully.
Throughout the book, he makes clear the many ways in which
he expects that he and his pastoral colleague disagree, and why
his rational, scientific, secular position is superior to what he
presumes the pastor believes. But still—he is asking for help.

This is a remarkable reversal from 1967, when Professor
Lynn White laid the blame for our modern ecological crisis at
the feet of Christianity in his essay, "The Historical Roots of our
Ecologic Crisis":

*... modern technology is at least partly to be explained as*
*an Occidental and voluntarist realizing of the Christian*
*dogma of man's transcendence of, and rightful mastery*
*over, nature. But, as we now recognize, somewhat over a*
*century ago science and technology—hitherto quite sep-*
*arate activities—joined to give mankind powers which,*
*to judge by man of the ecologic effects, are out of con-*
*trol.* ***If so, Christianity bears a huge burden of guilt.***
[White 1966, reprinted in R.J. Berry, ed, 2000, 40; emphasis mine].

It was not so, as numbers of writers have demonstrated in
the years since. Even White's assault on Christianity concluded

with an implicit recognition that, whatever the source of the problem, religion has to be part of the solution:

> *Since the roots of our trouble are so largely religious, the remedy must also be essentially religious, whether we call it that or not. We must rethink and refeel our nature and destiny. The profoundly religious, but heretical, sense of the primitive Franciscans for the spiritual autonomy of all parts of nature may point a direction. I propose Francis as a patron saint for ecologists.* [*Ibid*]

And now the tables have so turned that Wilson believes that "religion and science are the two most powerful forces in the world today" [Wilson, 2006, 5]. I am sure that he has in mind the power of influence—both popular and political. Evangelical Christians are said to have influence in the White House for the time being, though how real that influence is remains to be seen. Political questions aside, the possibility of popular influence is obvious. We have millions of people in church every Sunday. If we speak, people will listen. In this, Wilson is right—it would be no small thing to recruit the 30 million evangelicals in the US and many more around the world in a global effort to reverse the damage now being done to our world.

But the ability to influence people is not the only, or even the best role the Church can play. My convictions about the role of the Church in this crisis come from a belief that environmental problems are sin problems. There is an underlying spiritual dissonance in the universe that makes it impossible for us to live within our means and in harmony with the natural systems that support our lives. We are out of touch with the One who runs the place. This being the case, the most careful science and the best economic theories and the most profound governmental policies, while necessary, will never be enough. We have a spiritual problem, and we need a spiritual solution.

Applying biblical solutions to spiritual problems is what the church is all about, and that is what we can bring to the table in this crisis. We call it redemption—God's plan and provision to reconcile all things to himself, and it applies as much to our environmental crisis as it does to every other aspect of our lives. That this is not immediately evident in the current actions of the church is no surprise. We in the church have been moderately energetic in seeking to respond to many needs that we see in the world. We feed the hungry and we heal the sick. I have spent time personally in disaster response efforts, and I have seen that the most effective agencies for disaster relief are often Christian faith–based organizations. When we see and understand a need, we respond: enthusiastically, generously and usually effectively. But not, it seems, when it comes to environmental issues.

My experience has been like that of many others in this field. Simple conversations often reveal a serious disconnect between my view of the environmental crisis and that of many other evangelical Christians. During one business trip, I was visiting a local church. I was welcomed by a couple of members before the service began, who were friendly enough to ask me what brought me to their town. "I work with a Christian environmental organization,' I replied—and there was a long, long pause. "A what?"—another silence. "I didn't know there was such a thing." He not only didn't know it, but his eyes told me he wasn't too sure that it was possible. I wondered later if the particularly enthusiastic altar call at the end of the service was for me!

At the 2003 InterVarsity Urbana Convention—a great gathering of missionaries, mission organizations and students that is held every three years—I was Au Sable Institute's representative in the exhibit hall. I found myself besieged by students every day of the conference. It appeared that Au Sable was the only organization among hundreds present that had any ministry related to caring for the environment. Students could not believe this. They were Environmental Studies majors, Environmental Science majors, or just students who were aware of the environmental crisis and who saw it as one of the great needs of the day. They wanted to serve the Kingdom of God by working to address the abuse of God's creation that they could see all around them and all around the world. They could not understand why this problem, so apparent to them, seemed to not even exist in the world of Christian mission organizations.

This was the same problem Craig Sorley was experiencing in Kenya that led him to write to me. He wanted to "do environmental missions" the way many organizations "do medical missions". Where traditional medical missions works through clinics, hospitals and public health programs to share the good news of Jesus, he would 'heal the earth' through tree planting and similar projects. My wife Susanna and I prayed much about this opportunity, and finally, knowing the risks but believing God was guiding us toward an important new ministry, we decided to accept Craig's invitation. We worked together on a proposal for such an organization for the next few months, sought the advice of many friends and acquaintances, and the result was the birth of Care of Creation, Inc. in April 2005.

Our vision statement captures the goal we each had in mind when we began:

*Mobilizing the worldwide Church toward a
God-centered response to the environmental crisis*

- *That brings glory to the creator;*

- *Advances the cause of Christ;*

- *And leads to a transformation of the people
and the land that sustains them.*

You will notice that three-fourths of our mission statement has to do with God: We are looking for a 'God-centered' response that brings him glory and that advances the 'cause of Christ.' These are theological concepts that we are applying to very real and messy problems. The challenges presented by the environmental crisis are real: People are suffering and solutions will require us to get our hands dirty. We don't believe that Bible study can take the place of planting trees, or that theological propositions can mystically solve soil erosion. But we do believe that an approach to the environmental crisis that is theologically sound, scientifically informed and implemented by a community of redeemed people acting out of love for God and for each other—that is what the Church is, after all—can do what no one else has been able to do.

Care of Creation is off to a strong start. Craig's project in Kenya is in the process of encouraging churches and schools in many parts of the country to teach biblically based creation care, and to develop their own tree nurseries to provide seedlings for their people to plant. We are working to establish the week after Easter every year as a National Tree Planting week in celebration of the resurrection. And we have inquiries from all of the surrounding East African countries asking for our help to mobilize the Church in those countries as well.

We are excited about the work God has given us to do. But we are only one small organization trying to make an impact on one section of God's wonderful world. Our work is focused on Africa—for that is the piece of God's creation where we see great needs and great opportunities to turn the crisis around. But this book is not about our organization—it is about the whole Church, God's people everywhere, waking up to the problems and opportunities represented by the environmental crisis we see in the world today. The problems in Kenya are repeated in Southeast Asia and Latin America, and the Church is strong in these places. We see great possibilities if the Church in the USA, Canada, and other "developed' countries were to mobilize. After all, much of the damage to the globe originates in these countries, even though the effects are being felt far away.

We use the term 'mobilization' by design. It carries a certain military connotation that helps convey urgency. But mobilizing something also suggests a deployment of resources that already exist, and that is an important part of my thesis. The Church needs to change little to be effective in the environmental crisis. We have the beliefs, we have the people, we have programs in place. We don't need to invent anything—we simply need to go to work. Let's open the warehouse doors and move out the equipment.

A word on the structure of the book: In Chapter One I will outline the current environmental crisis in broad strokes. It is a crisis that in some respects is different than what we faced in 1970, and much more frightening. You will note immediately that this is not a book about climate change; though that is a significant part of the crisis we are facing, the climate change discussion generates more heat than light. To some it may seem that if the climate change prognosticators are wrong, we can relax. Nothing could be further from the truth. Even if climate advocates are wrong—and this seems less likely by the day— God's creation is still in deep trouble, and so I have chosen to make the arguments without a great deal of emphasis on that particular issue.

The Church is a theological organization; in secular terms, we could say that it is "values-based". It is my belief, confirmed in my own experience, that biblical principles that are broadly accepted among evangelicals contain a ready–made foundation for a response to the environmental crisis. Chapters 2–6 are a discussion of a few of the major doctrines that are important in this regard: Creation, incarnation, sin, redemption and the Church. Other doctrines could have been included; these, to me, form a solid and powerful argument that the Church can— and must—respond to the environmental crisis by actively caring for God's creation.

The more perceptive reader will note that one doctrine I have not covered is eschatology—end times, the return of Jesus at the end of history. This may seem odd, as one of the arguments sometimes posed against caring for creation is that "it's all going to burn up anyway." This is hardly a serious point of view, and usually evaporates with a simple analogy. I will sometimes pretend to hand such a person a pack of cigarettes and ask them, quite seriously, why they don't smoke. "Your body is just going to die anyway—and rot in the grave. So why not?" We know we have to care for our bodies, as temporary as they are, and almost everyone understands immediately that the same logic applies to caring for creation. However, the main reason I've skipped this doctrine in this book is that I'm not quite ready to wade into that discussion. Is the "New Earth" of Revelation a "brand-new" earth as many of us have assumed? Or is it a redeemed earth—"remade' and "recycled'—as the language of I Peter in particular seems to suggest? I am concerned that, like the climate change discussion, a chapter on eschatology at this point would generate lots of heat and not as much light as I would like.

Chapters 7–12 discuss the mobilization of the Church in practical terms, from worship and education to facilities and the missions program. Remember the term, "Mobilization'. We want to activate resources that are already in place. Much of what is needed is already present in almost every congregation or church fellowship. Your own church has a variety of activities and programs now underway that can be powerful instruments in a response to the environmental crisis. Adding creation care need not displace any programs that already exist. Think of it rather as a 'mix-in' (as in one of those gourmet ice cream shops) that will enrich every aspect of church life it touches—and save scarce ministry dollars as well. No family ever lost money saving energy—and no church has grown poorer or more stretched because it chose to emphasize creation care throughout its range of ministry activities.

The final chapter is a brief appeal to the people who will be key in the mobilization of the church: Pastors, ordinary church members, and particularly students. If the Church (uppercase C) is to mobilize, it will only happen if many churches (lower case c) become concerned and active—and this will only happen if individual people decide that this is important enough to do something about. For in the end, a church is what its members are, and a church does what its members decide to do.

*Part 1:  The Message*

# one

## RUNNING ON EMPTY

Earth Day, 1970. In the industrial town of Fitchburg, Massachusetts, I am about to make my public speaking debut. I'm a junior in High School, and I've been drafted by my home room teacher. His name, face and my speech are lost to history, but the event is not. This was the first Earth Day, and it could not have come too soon for this place. Fitchburg was at that time a paper mill town. The local mills had been long accustomed to using the Nashua River that runs through the center of town as a convenient outlet for their waste. We teenagers were illogically proud of the fact that the river changed color by the day, depending on what color paper was being manufactured upstream. While I have no recollection as to what I actually said at that school assembly thirty some years ago, I am very much aware of the difference Earth Day has made in Fitchburg, and in the country.

Thanks to that first Earth Day, and the attention paid to it by legislators in Washington, a raft of legislation was passed requiring clean air, clean water, and concessions for species that were in danger of extinction. Evidence for the success of that effort is everywhere—in Fitchburg and around the country. Today you could swim in the Nashua River. Knowing what I know of its history, I wouldn't recommend it—but still, you could.

The environmental crisis seems to be over. Solved in 1970. Many of the rivers are clean, and most are at least cleaner than they were. The bald eagle is no longer a rarity and has been removed from the endangered species list. The gray wolf, one of our national symbols of wilderness, has recovered from the brink of extinction. Its howls can be heard from Michigan to Washington State, and it may soon be removed from the endangered species list. As I write these words, it is a glorious fall day in southern Wisconsin. I live in an 'inner suburb' of a medium size city. I am surrounded by about 200,000 other human beings, but there is little if any evidence of an 'environmental crisis' that I can see. "God's in his heaven, all's right with the world" would sum things up quite nicely: The sky is blue, with white puffy clouds. The air is just a bit chill, with the promise of frost in a couple of weeks. Bright yellow leaves on some of the trees stand out against the dark green of some of their fellows who have not yet felt the coming of winter. High overhead an occasional "V" of geese meanders toward the south. What environmental crisis?

*More than meets the eye*

Unfortunately, things aren't always as they appear. If you were to join me in the dining room of my duplex, we could look out over the back deck, across a small cul-de-sac, and see between two other houses what looks like a lovely restored prairie, perhaps 200 yards from my house. It is home to a variety of birds, small mammals and many creatures I've never met. To our left, behind a tall clump of trees, is a small pond that hosts ducks and geese, and probably a few fish, though no neighborhood child has to my knowledge ever succeeded in catching any. A bike trail winds past the prairie, around the pond, and connects with one of the best city bike trail systems in the Midwest. I could ride nine miles to the center of Madison and only spend one mile of that distance on city streets. Or I could walk a block and catch a city bus that would take me to the same place in about the same amount of time. It would appear that I am living in a perfect example of a modern urban/suburban development that has kept in touch with nature. There are people everywhere. But there are still trees, green grass and even a restored prairie.

What you don't know is that the restored prairie covers a former city dump. An innocent looking utility building to the right, just out of sight from our deck vantage point, is a sophisticated methane recovery system that runs night and day. It was installed after a house just like mine exploded a number of years ago. Neighbors still talk about it. It appears that methane from the dump infiltrated the basement and found its way to the furnace or water heater pilot light. No one was home at the time, but the resulting explosion was spectacular. Even now, if you purchase a house bordering the 'prairie', you will inherit a thick set of documents advising you that, while the city is doing its best to protect you by collecting methane from the unseen waste, there are no guarantees that your house will not explode like the first one did.

### An Invisible Crisis

That restored prairie is a parable of the environmental crisis in America today. Like that prairie, the environmental crisis is hidden from most Americans. We took care of the colored rivers—and those that tended to catch fire. The majority of us can still see green grass, we can attract birds to our feeders, and most days for most of us the air is tolerably breathable. So, mostly, things don't look so bad. But we might want to remember that you can't see the methane until it explodes.

Yes, we still have a crisis. In some parts of the world, it is all too visible, as if the dump behind my house had never been covered at all. And the results are often tragic for the people who live there. In late September 2004 Hurricane Jeanne, the fifth major storm of that year's hurricane season, ravaged the Caribbean and eastern United States. Millions of people were affected, and the storm caused substantial damage everywhere. But the casualty figures are stunning: Jeanne killed five people in the continental US, seven in Puerto Rico, 18 in the Dominican Republic, but more than 3,000 in Haiti. Why? Much more than other countries affected, Haiti has suffered catastrophic environmental damage. Less than one per cent of Haiti's forest is intact, and without trees to hold back soil and absorb rainfall, even modest showers can turn into mudslides. Jeanne's thirteen inches of rain on the mountains above the city of Gonaives caused a mud-avalanche that affected 80,000 people.

But even in North America, problems like my hidden city dump still exist. You can't see that underground water levels are dropping—but they are, between 30 and 300 feet per year everywhere from Kansas and Nebraska to China and India. The green lawns and beautiful golf courses we take as a sign of health and beauty are a product of chemical poisons that contribute to the destruction of vast numbers of creatures. Even our blankets and frying pans are the source of hundreds of manmade chemicals in our bloodstreams.

Wilson sums up the situation in this way:

> ...humanity is already the first species in the history of life to become a geophysical force. We have, all by our bipedal, wobbly headed selves, altered Earth's atmosphere and climate away from the norm. We have spread thousands of toxic chemicals worldwide, appropriated 40% of the solar energy available for photosynthesis, converted almost all of the easily arable land, dammed most of the rivers, raised the planet sea level, and now, in a manner likely to get everyone's attention like nothing else before

*it, we are close to running out of fresh water. A collateral of all of this frenetic activity is the continuing extinction of wild ecosystems, along with the species that compose them. This happens to be the only human impact that is irreversible.* [Wilson 2006, 29]

## A different kind of crisis

Today's crisis is qualitatively different from that which we faced thirty five years ago. The problems we were facing then, though widespread, were essentially local in nature. One river or watershed was contaminated and could be fixed. One city had substandard air quality, and regulations could be imposed. What is clear now is that the crisis we face is global. It is world-wide in extent, and interconnected systems that we do not even understand are being impacted. Globalization is not new— God's biosphere has always functioned globally. All parts are connected, and human impact has increased to the point that the entire system is under threat. Every local problem is caused by or causes problems in other corners of the world. Loss of rain forest cover in the Amazon affects climate in North America and Europe. Toxic air pollution in China descends in the rain of California and Oregon. Chemicals pumped into the atmosphere around the world show up in the blood and breast milk of people living above the Arctic Circle.

Even yesterday's local problems turn out to have global complications. In 1970, the concern of the citizens of Fitchburg, Massachusetts, was for the health of the Nashua River. It was a local problem. The cause was nearby. The solution seemed easy—reroute or treat the industrial waste. In actual fact, presumably at least partly in response to new regulations, most of the paper mills closed. Paper is still being produced, and rivers are probably still changing colors—but now the rivers have Chinese or Indonesian names.

Several additional factors make today's crisis different from any we have experienced before:

## People, People Everywhere

*It is a population crisis.* As I write, the United States has welcomed its 300 millionth resident. No one is sure if the newcomer is an infant or an arrival at Kennedy airport with two suitcases and a work permit. But it is instructive to note that Atlanta attorney Bobby Woo, whom Life Magazine designated the two hundred millionth American when he was born in November, 1967, is only 39 years old. In his lifetime, world population has approximately doubled, from 3 billion to 6 billion people. Quite simply, there are more people alive on earth now than ever before.

As Christians, we place a high value on human life. Every person is precious in God's sight—all are created in his image. The Bible applied universal dignity and meaning to the life of every human being long before the American Declaration of Independence enshrined the concept of "inalienable rights". Because of this, Christians may face a dilemma: How can we confront the problems raised by increasing numbers of precious people and still recognize and honor each one's uniqueness and dignity?

Some suggest that our increased population doesn't have to be a problem. For example, Japan is a country that appears to have managed a high population density and has maintained high standards of living and good environmental quality all at the same time. The question is this: Can anyone reasonably foresee an entire globe with the population density of Japan and with the same high economic and environmental standards. It's not going to happen. Here's why.

Strong governmental leadership, an economic base that can support technological solutions and the motivation of living on an island are all factors that may contribute to Japan's environmental success. But Japan is an exception—and even this 'environmental success story' is not quite as clear as it appears at first glance. Managing a large, high density population requires a disciplined society and an efficient, responsive and uncorrupt government. You may recall the book, Cheaper By the Dozen. No, not the recent movies—the book, written in 1948 by Frank Gilbreth, Jr. and his sister, Ernestine Gilbreth Carey, about their experiences growing up in a household of twelve children. The means to the family's survival  and the source of much hilarity in the story—was Dad's application of industrial efficiency techniques to family life:

> *Dad installed process and work charts in the bathrooms. Every child old enough to write—and Dad expected his offspring to start writing at a tender age—was required to initial the charts in the morning after he had brushed his teeth, taken a bath, combed his hair, and made his bed. At night, each child had to weigh himself, plot the figure on a graph, and initial the process charts again after he had done his homework, washed his hands and face and brushed his teeth. Mother wanted to have a place on the charts for saying prayers, but Dad said as far as he was concerned prayers were voluntary.*

> *It was regimentation, all right. But bear in mind the trouble most parents have in getting just one child off to school, and multiply it by twelve. Some regimentation was necessary to prevent bedlam . . .*
> [Gilbreth 1948, 2-3]

A family of 12 children was able to run smoothly because of tight discipline and careful management. It's the same way with countries: True, Japan has done it, but discipline and careful management are in short supply in every country where population is a serious problem.

The Japanese experience, however, is also misleading.  In some ways it parallels my story about Fitchburg.  Fitchburg cleaned its river by exporting the pollution to other places when the local paper mills closed. Japan would not be able to maintain its environmental or economic standards if she were not taking resources from—and exporting the accompanying problems to—other countries. Japan has maintained and enjoyed extensive forests at home, but is one of the major sources of tropical deforestation in countries like Indonesia. Japan's appetite for ocean seafood is voracious, and while she is not alone in this, the world's oceans are showing the strain. Japan's wood and fish have to come from somewhere.

Recent figures show that as many as sixteen countries have stable or declining populations. These include Ukraine, with a fertility rate of 1.1 births per woman (2.1 is "replacement rate'), Russia 1.2, Spain, 1.3, Japan, Germany, Italy and Romania at 1.3 and so on. Even China makes this list now, with a fertility rate of 1.8. All of this is encouraging, and has allowed some experts to revise population projections downward from as high as 12 billion in 2050 to "as low as" 8 billion. Keep in mind that "as low as" still requires us to accomodate about five times the current population of the United States before the population as a whole begins to stabilize. There are two reasons why stable or declining populations in some countries do not mean the problem has gone away. Even in these countries, many women are not of childbearing age, and therefore have not yet had their babies. This is like a movie theater that has distributed a number of coupons for free tickets. They have to calculate not only those already in the theater, but all of those who are holding tickets but haven't arrived yet.

The other big problem is one of distribution. While sixteen countries have stable fertility rates, many more do not. The Earth Policy Institute lists 33 countries—as of 2002—with fertility rates ranging from 2.3 (Vietnam) to 7.0 (Democratic Republic of Congo). It is by no means clear that people in the countries which are growing more crowded will be able to move to countries facing population shortages or that they will be welcome

when they arrive. Anti-immigration initiatives throug
developed world would tend to suggest that the "so
redistributing population is not going to be easy.

A friend of mine has a small summer cottage in northern
Michigan. Through unfortunate planning when the house was
built, it has an undersized septic tank situated close to a neighboring pond. When there aren't many people staying at the
house, the system can keep up with the demands placed on
it  that is, it can handle perhaps 2 showers and five or six toilet flushes in a twenty–four hour period. Anything more than
that, watch out! When more than two people are using the toilet
and taking showers, the tank fills and backs up into the house,
causing more than a little inconvenience. The world's population situation is like my friend's septic tank problem. His house
might have beds for five, ten or fifteen people, but that doesn't
matter. If the plumbing can't handle all those people, there is no
point trying to fill all of the beds. If by some measures the earth
could support many more people than it now does, by other,
more fundamental measures the system is already overloaded.
The plumbing is backing up.

The overload appears in two opposite but equally problem-
atic ways.


## Too much of a good thing


*It is a prosperity crisis.* We are witnessing a remarkable and
unprecedented transformation of economics, business and culture in the world today. Tom Friedman, New York Times colum-
nist and author of *The World is Flat* and *The Lexus and the Olive
Tree*, has watched and analyzed what is now known as globalization as well as anyone:

> ... *the force that gives [globalization] its unique character-
> is the newfound power for individuals to collaborate and*

*compete globally. . . . The flat-world platform is the prod-
uct of a convergence of the personal computer (which allowed every individual to suddenly become the author of
his or her own content in digital form) with fiber optic
cable (which suddenly allowed all those individuals to
access more and more digital content around the world
for next to nothing) with the rise of work flow software
(which enabled individuals all over the world to collabo-
rate on that same digital content from anywhere, regard-
less of the distances between them). No one anticipated
this convergence. It just happened- right around the year
2000.* [Friedman 2004, 9-11]

Globalization has been controversial but no one questions
that it is real and it is here. While it has not, and cannot, eliminate global poverty, it has brought the possibility of a western-
style, consumer oriented lifestyle within the reach of millions
of people around the world, particularly in India and China,
and this more quickly than anyone thought possible.

What is ironic is that a unified global economy that brings
prosperity to millions who have been previously left out could
sink the entire global ship—or, to switch metaphors, bring down
the global airliner: Last year I traveled a lot as I worked on
the Pakistan earthquake. Because I was alone and was traveling frequently, I was able to travel light, usually with just
one suitcase to check. This was not true of many of my fellow passengers. Every time I checked in, I watched as one or
another unfortunate family learned that they could not bring
all of the suitcases they wanted to. The cases were too heavy,
or there were too many of them, or (often) both. I sympathized
with them—I've been there myself at times—but I also understood why the airlines have limitations on baggage. If everyone brings everything they want, the plane will never get off
the ground. This in fact happened on one of the flights I was to
take. I saw a mountain of luggage to one side of the baggage
hall, and learned that the previous flight had been overweight

and all of this baggage had been removed and would have to go on another flight. Such limits are written into the laws of the physical universe. They determine that a line has to be drawn, or the results will be catastrophic.

Our global economy is like one of those planes. We've had a few passengers—primarily those of us living in North America and Europe—who have been traveling with 20 or 30 suitcases each. We've been able to get away with it because most of the passengers in the rear of the plane haven't had any luggage at all. The unlooked for arrival of globalization means more and more of these passengers are able to bring five, seven or ten suitcases of their own. The result is easily predictable: The capacity of this plane is rapidly running out.

The World Wildlife Fund recently released a report estimating that the human race as whole was exceeding the sustainable capacity of the earth by 25% in 2003, the most recent year for which statistics were available. Estimates are that in 2006, we will have been using 30%, and that this pattern will increase to an annual rate of 100% by 2050. Consider the consumption rates anticipated for just one country, China. According to author Lester Brown, if the Chinese economy continues to expand at current rates, and if Chinese consumers attain levels of personal consumption similar to those in the United States, in 25 years, China will need [Brown 2006, 10]:

- Two-thirds of the world's entire current grain harvest;

- Double the world's current manufacturing capacity of paper;

- 99 million barrels of oil per day (total global production is now 'only' 84 million barrels per day)

Obviously, such a situation is not sustainable. The world cannot support an entire globe of people living at the standard Americans and Europeans take for granted. But they are trying to, and will continue to do so until we all agree on how much we can each bring on board.

*Not enough of anything*

Paradoxically, the global environmental crisis is also a poverty crisis. For every new consumer seeking to benefit from the new prosperity of globalization, there are dozens or hundreds doomed to lives of utter misery. Dickens' line, "it was the best of times, it was the worst of times" may never have been as starkly true as it is today. In too many countries, too many people are trying to eke a living out of plots of land that are simply too small and too depleted to support human beings any longer.

The staff of my organization, Care of Creation, reported recently from a meeting with several farmers in the small village of Tiekunu, Kenya, near the edge of the Rift Valley. These farmers have been cultivating the same family plots for more than 30 years. We asked them what typical harvests were like in 1975, compared with 2006. This is what we learned (a 'bag' is a large burlap sack that would hold several bushels):

- Corn production in 1975 was 30 bags/acre, today 7 bags/acre

- Bean production in 1975, 20 bags/acre, today 5 bags/acre

- Potato production in 1975, 100 bags/acre, today 10 bags/acre

This is in an area where more people need to live off the same plots of land—in some cases, many more people. Such agricultural statistics indicate both the result of environmental damage to the soil, and a certain prediction of more to come, as poverty stricken families force the land to try to produce more and more with less and less. The end result is not hard to picture: While the wealthy in the front of the plane threaten it by loading on more and more suitcases, the poor at the back scrape the very insulation off the wires in an attempt to survive.

The challenges are not simply due to attempts to squeeze more people onto ancient family farms, however. The arrival of globalization sometimes does bring prosperity—but often it means environmental disaster instead. This dark side of global prosperity has allowed large corporations to easily move their businesses anywhere they wish around the world. Sometimes they are looking for lower wages; in other cases, the corporate ideal is little or no environmental regulation. The result is that prosperous consumers of North America and Europe are able to keep their local environments clean by exporting the toxic effects of modern manufacturing to other communities that are in desperate need of jobs.

Rural China is an easy example, though people in every other "less developed" country are in the same situation. We see frequent news reports from China reporting toxic spills in major rivers affecting millions of people, including one in 2005 that may have involved more than 100 tons of benzene, an industrial solvent, released into the Songhua river. What may be even more tragic are reports now coming out of other areas in rural China where chronic pollution is causing massive increases in cancer and other environmentally triggered diseases, some of which are caused by toxic metals from electronic components shipped from the US and Europe for recycling.

*A 'perfect storm'*

Inevitably, the perfect storm' of population, prosperity and poverty is resulting in a global political crisis. Politics is the way we human beings manage our public affairs, and it would be foolish not to expect that an environmental crisis of such proportions would spill over into the political realm. We occasionally worry about political threats arising from specific environmental problems, such as water wars in the Middle East that are a real potential threat in that region that is beset by so many other tensions as well. However, a bigger threat is the overall level of stress that environmentally devastated countries experience, creating internal tensions that often cause or contribute to international disputes and even international terrorism.

A list of the countries experiencing environmental stress (like Afghanistan, Haiti, Indonesia, Nepal, Pakistan, Rwanda and Somalia, to name just a few) would be almost identical to a list of those experiencing the greatest political tensions domestically and with their neighbors. We can choose to solve environmental problems, or they can be left to solve themselves, according to author Jared Diamond. One way or another, they will be resolved:

> *The only question is whether they will become resolved in pleasant ways of our own choice, or in unpleasant ways not of our choice, such as warfare, genocide, starvation, disease epidemics, and collapses of societies. While all of those grim phenomena have been endemic to humanity throughout our history, **their frequency increases with environmental degradation, population pressure, and the resulting poverty and instability.***
> [Diamond 2005, 498; emphasis mine]

> *When people are desperate, undernourished, and without hope, they blame their governments, which they see as responsible for or unable to solve their problems. They try to emigrate at any cost. They fight each other over land. They kill each other. They start civil wars. They figure they have nothing to lose, so they become terrorists, or they support or tolerate terrorism.*
> [Diamond 2005, 516]

I am sure we all agree that it is much better to resolve the problems we have been describing "in pleasant ways of our own choice" rather than to allow these things to resolve themselves. But what does that mean? It means discussion, cooperation, and compromise. It means looking beyond and behind the symptoms that present themselves in order to find underlying causes. It means having the imagination to come up with original solutions for unprecedented problems, and the courage to propose and carry out those solutions. In a word, it means leadership. Our political crisis is a leadership crisis.

The world is crying out for people who can address the challenges of population, prosperity, poverty and politics with imagination and with courage—people who can identify the problems and apply real and lasting solutions, for corruption, ignorance and fear obscure both the real problem and the real solution—a solution that has not been tried very often. It has to do with God.

# BY HIM AND FOR HIM

As I sit at my desk, I can see a set of three hand-made mugs. They are not high art, but they're attractive and functional. The artist who made them claims they are dishwasher safe. They could sell for a decent price in the kind of store that sells hand-made pottery.

But these mugs are not for sale. And I don't think I will be using them very often, if at all. Why? Because I know who made them. I have a special relationship with her and these mugs remind me of her, especially now that she's no longer a daily part of my life. She's my youngest daughter. I could show you, in various corners of my house, all kinds of other things that one or another of my four children have made, and that are special for that reason alone. There is the most unusual set of salt and pepper shaker you've ever seen in the kitchen, and a treasure trove of first, second or third grade papers and awards in boxes in the basement. These are plainly useless and, to you, worthless as well. But my wife and I keep them. Why? These things—mugs, papers, drawings, award certificates—are all part of relationships. I value them because I value the people who made them.

The biggest reason for caring for God's creation has nothing to do with the extent or the severity of the crisis, the number of people affected or even the ultimate future of the human race. It has to do with one simple fact: I know the God who made it all. And I love him. If I can place a high price on things that have little or no objective value simply because they were made by one of my children, how much more ought I to value and care for this amazing world God made—this world that is precious because he made it, and that represents an excellence and beauty far beyond anything that any of us could begin to comprehend, let alone make on our own.

### "Who" matters

The first verses of Genesis tell us that God made the world, but do not tell us much else. We don't know how, we don't know when. We actually can get a better handle on God's creative process from Paul's letter to the Colossians:

> [Jesus Christ] is the image of the invisible God, the first-born over all creation. For by him, all things were created: things in heaven and on earth, visible and invisible, whether thrones or powers or rulers or authorities; all things were created by him and for him. He is before all things, and in him all things hold together.
> [Colossians 1:15-17]

It wasn't "just God" who created—as if there could be "just God". Nor, if we were dividing tasks among members of the Trinity, would it be God the Father. The agent of creation was Jesus—the person who came, lived among us, died and rose from the dead—the One who saved us from our sins. He is the Creator: "by him all things were created." He is the sustainer of creation—the force that holds all things together, whatever that means. And he is the reason for creation: "all things were created...for him."

And this Person, whom John calls "Logos", Greek for "The Word" (John 1:1) is the One I call my Savior. The relationship here is much closer than my relationship with the maker of the mugs on my desk. If I call myself a Christian or a Christ-follower, I am following the One who made everything. The One for whom everything was created. The One who holds all of the molecules in everything together. "Everything" means me. And you. Your family members. The neighbor across the street. My dog. Your cat and your parakeets and the rabbits and squirrels in the yard. The dandelions and creeping Charlie that decorate my lawn. The glorious fall leaves and the deep blue sky and last night's full moon and the earthworms and microbes and stars and constellations.

I know who made every piece of creation in the reach of my fingers and my mind. I love him because he died for me and called me to have a special relationship with him. How can I not love the things he has made?

### And "Why" matters, too

"Environmental Stewardship". This is one of the most common phrases used today to talk about taking care of the earth. I like it, particularly because of the second word in it. A steward, according to my dictionary, is someone who takes care of something on behalf of someone else.

As it happens, the house next to mine is owned by a landlord. Joe (not his real name) owns the property, but lives elsewhere in the city and rents the apartments to tenants. He is a good landlord, and even does the mowing and snow removal himself. But he recently took a new job that has given him much less time to tend the property, and so he is in the process of looking for a property manager to take care of it for him. What he is looking for is a "steward", someone who understands what he wants to do with his house, and will manage it accordingly.

Many people who use the term "stewardship" do so without knowing or believing in God, and that is technically possible. A secular environmentalist may see herself as a steward and may teach and encourage what she calls environmental stewardship. She will probably mean either that she is caring for the earth on behalf of future (human) generations, or on behalf of the earth and its creatures themselves. Either is a legitimate use of the concept of stewardship, and if you do not believe there is a God, stewardship of this kind is an acceptable and necessary moral principle.

But I am a Christian, I do believe in God, and for me, therefore, there is a richness and depth to the concept of stewardship that goes far, far beyond these. When I say that I am a "steward", I see myself as someone taking care of God's property on his behalf. He did not make this world for me—he made it for himself. But he put me—us—here to take care of it. Just as my friend Joe is looking for a property manager who will take care of his property with his goals in mind, you and I cannot be effective stewards of God's property until we understand what his goals are. This brings up the question, what are his goals? Why did he make it all in the first place? Why is it here?

The secularist—environmentalist or not—has no answer to this question. Maybe he or she doesn't need one. There is no "why"—the world just happens to be here. But even they would have to admit that it takes a bit of the wind out of the moral imperative that any ethic needs. If there is no "why", the world might just as easily happen not to be here, and how long it lasts doesn't really matter one way or another. The secular stewardship ethic begins to falter. If there is no discernible reason for the existence of present or future generations of humans, or for the presence of other species, acting as a steward on their behalf is a nice thought, but in the end, who is really going to care if those future generations exist and prosper or not?

As a Christian, I can legitimately ask why he made all that he made, and I can expect an answer. There is an answer that opens vistas of meaning for us, and that lends a powerful impetus to our role and actions as his property managers. The answer is implicit in one of the thoughts we have already seen in Colossians 1:16: He made it, not for us, but for himself.

*A temple carved out of space...*

Let's think about those first chapters of Genesis. Professor John Walton (Wheaton College) suggests, with some other commentators, that the climax of God's creative acts is not on day six, when he creates man and woman (Genesis 1:26); it is day seven, when God finished his work and blessed it:

> *The cosmos is not set up with only people in mind. The cosmos is also intended to carry out a function related to God. On the seventh day we discover that God has been working to achieve a rest. This seventh day is not a theological appendix to the creation account, just to bring closure now that the main event of creating people has been reported. It intimates the purpose of creation and of the cosmos. God not only sets up the cosmos so that people will have a place;* **he also sets up the cosmos to serve as his temple...** *He is making a rest for himself, a rest provided for by the completed cosmos. Inhabiting his resting place is the equivalent to being enthroned—it is connected to taking up his role as sovereign ruler of the cosmos. The temple simply provides a symbolic reality for this concept.* [Walton 2001, 148; emphasis mine]

"He sets up the cosmos to serve as his temple." A temple in any culture is a place where people meet their God or gods and where they go to worship. It is usually a building, and the functions that occur there—prayer, worship, confession, sacrifice—are all designed to help the worshipers develop and pursue a relationship of some kind with the deity to whom the temple is dedicated. Temples are platforms for divine/human interaction. They are made for relationship.

That's what the biblical story is about: God's relationship with the human race. God created us "in his image" so that he could have a relationship with us. This relationship was perfect in the Garden of Eden, was broken at the fall, was restored by Jesus on the Cross. The whole story is about relationships—and particularly about God's patience and pursuit of a fallen humanity through the corridors of history. And that relationship had to have a place in which it could be played out. That place is creation. That is why we can say that the cosmos is a temple. That is why God created creation.

### Not divine, but sacred

Does it matter? Absolutely. One of the concerns I hear expressed among Christians when we talk about environmental issues is a fear of "worshiping" creation. An early book on this subject by Tony Campolo was called *How to Rescue the Earth without Worshiping Nature*. When we understand that God made creation as a temple, this problem takes care of itself.

While I was working on the Pakistan earthquake in late 2005 and early 2006, I was based in Islamabad, Pakistan's capital city. My home and office was within sight of the Faisal Mosque, Islamabad's most prominent landmark, Pakistan's equivalent to Washington's National Cathedral. Located on the edge of the city, tucked against the Margallah hills, this mosque is an important landmark and a popular tourist attraction. I took visitors there on several occasions, and would often walk the grounds on my own early in the morning or in the evening.

The outside courtyard of Faisal mosque is a marble-paved square about 150 yards on each side, and the worship area is comprised of a single hall approximately 80 yards square. Four minarets stand about 150 feet high at each corner of the main worship pavilion. Visitors are permitted to wander throughout the complex—the worship hall is closed except during prayer times—and tourists, men and women alike, are welcome, with just two conditions imposed on both Muslims and non-Muslims: Women should cover their heads, and everyone must remove their shoes. Why? The structure is not divine. A Muslim would shudder at the thought. Even a hint of idolatry is anathema in Islam. No, it is not divine, but it is a sacred place. It has been built, and set apart, for the worship of God and must therefore be treated with special respect.

You will find the same thing if you visit the great cathedrals of Europe. You won't be asked to remove your shoes or cover your head, but you will find that the crowds of tourists, though they are on holiday, will move about quietly and will speak in low, respectful voices. We understand that these are special places—and we treat them with reverence.

So with God's creation. It is all holy ground, not just the area around Moses' burning bush. All of it is "worship space" because that is why God created it: to be a place where he could relate to his people. We should, and we must, respect it and care for it: Not because it is divine, but because it is sacred in the same way that a temple, cathedral or mosque is sacred. It is a place to meet God.

Do you ever wonder why it is easier to worship God outside, under the trees or on a mountain top or beneath the stars on a summer night? It's because that is why God made it all. He designed it to point to himself, so that you and I would find it easy—or easier—to worship him, pray to him, and hear his voice speaking to us. Dorothy Frances Gurney's poem contains deep truth:

> *The kiss of the sun for pardon,*
> *The song of the birds for mirth,*
> *One is nearer God's heart in a garden*
> *Than anywhere else on earth.*

### Slave masters or choirmasters?

One of the great misunderstandings of scripture—for which thousands of creatures have paid dearly—arises from what is known as the dominion teaching of Genesis 1:

> *Let them rule (have dominion) over the fish of the sea and*
> *the birds of the air, over the livestock, over all the earth,*
> *and over all the creatures that move along the ground.*
> [Genesis 1:26]

This has been used by Christians to justify abuse of nature, and by skeptics who use it to criticize believers—sometimes justly, sometimes not. There is no need for us to replay this long argument—several of the books listed at the end of this one will give you all the background you want. I would like to suggest, though, that if we understand God's purpose in creation properly, this problem, like the last, will disappear.

Let's pick up the worship motif again. It turns out that we are not the only actors in this great worship space. The author of Psalm 148 describes creation as an active participant in the worship of God. All of God's creatures, from the angels and the heavenly hosts to the inanimate creation (sun and moon, waters above, ocean depths, mountains and hills); from small creatures and flying birds to all of the human race,

*Praise the Lord from the earth, you great sea creatures
  and all ocean depths,*
*Lightning and hail, snow and clouds, stormy winds that
  do his bidding,*
*You mountains and all hills, fruit trees and cedars, wild
  animals and all cattle,*
*Small creatures and flying birds, kings of the earth and
  all nations,*
*You princes and all rulers on earth, young men and maid-
  ens, old men and children.*
*Let them praise the name of the Lord, for his name alone
  is exalted;*
*His splendor is above the earth and the heavens.*
[Psalm 148:7-13]

For more like this, read Psalm 19, Psalm 104, Job 38, 39 and
40. Consider the example of Jesus (Luke 4:42) and some of his
teachings (Matthew 6:26ff).There is no shortage of scriptures
describing the role creation plays in worshiping God its creator.

The temple is unique, because it is animate. This psalm
makes me think of a children's cartoon. You know the kind I
mean: The furniture comes to life and the teapot dances with
the tea cups. God's temple isn't just a place for worship—it
participates in that worship. This is what Jesus was talking
about when his enemies complained about the way the crowds
were treating him. Their enthusiastic praise seemed to border
on blasphemous worship. Jesus' response to the complaints:
"If they (the crowds) keep quiet, the stones will cry out." (Luke
19:40)

This means creation is both temple and choir. And this
adds an important layer of meaning to the concept of "dominion". The purpose of our leadership over creation is not that
we might take anything we want from the riches of the earth
for our own selfish purposes. No! We are the choirmasters.

Our job is to lead the cosmic choir that inhabits the temple of creation.

One of my regrets in life is that I was born with little musical ability. I can appreciate good music, and I can carry the melody of a song if I have a lot of help around me. I just don't have the ear/voice coordination that natural musicians have. But I have a friend with amazing musical abilities. He's been a pastor of music and worship in several large churches and I have followed his career with interest. Tom (not his real name) is a classical, concert level musician in his own right. But his real gift goes beyond his ability to produce music himself. His special talent is the way he can draw music out of others, often far beyond what they think they can accomplish. That is the measure of a true choirmaster—someone who draws music out of a choir that no one knew was there, not even the members of the choir themselves.

This is what "dominion" ought to mean. Yes, God has made us leaders and rulers. And our rulership has one purpose: To lead the cosmic choir in worship of the creator. In light of this, the quality of our leadership needs to be called into serious question. The choir is dying, and we are responsible. One in eight species of birds is threatened with extinction, as is one in four mammals, and an unknown number of fish. Half of amphibians will not be on earth within the next decade or two—can you imagine the choir of creation without frogs? Places for creatures to live disappear as the surface of the earth is covered by houses and pavement, highways and cities, poisons filter into their water, and whole mountains are destroyed to find veins of coal hidden beneath. This is dominion as domination, not dominion as stewardship. It is not improving the worship coming from the choir. What kind of choirmasters are we, when the choir is being destroyed under our own hands?

## The Book of God's Works

I recently talked with a friend who lives in North Carolina, across the street from a large Baptist church, the kind that is loudly committed to 'saving the lost'. Part of the church's property included a lovely section of woods with a stream. Mary (not her real name) doesn't worship at that church but she used to spend a great deal of time in those woods, watching the birds, worshiping and praying. Last year the church needed more parking space. (You can see what is coming, can't you?) They removed the woods for a new parking lot. Doing so, they failed to protect the stream during construction and it was destroyed as well. More people can now park their cars, and go inside to hear sermons about God's love. I can almost hear them singing, "His eye is on the sparrow, I know he cares for me…" Meanwhile, outside their sanctuary, God's great worship space has fewer places for sparrows to live, and one of God's chapels for prayer and worship is gone. Mary is not necessarily farther from God because of this—but she certainly is not closer to the church across the street.

This incident is more common than not. And it is the result of one more error we often make, when we fail to realize that God made creation to be one of the primary means by which human beings could come to know him. My friend and former boss, Dr. Calvin DeWitt, often speaks of the value of an upbringing that allowed him to study the "book of God's word" and "the book of God's works" together. Psalm 19 is a hymn of praise to God for revealing himself to us, and half of the Psalm—the first half, incidentally—is given to God's revelation of himself in nature:

*The heavens declare the glory of God,*
*The skies proclaim the work of his hands.*
*Day after day they pour forth speech;*

*Night after night they display knowledge.*
*There is no speech or language where their voice is not*
    *heard.*
*Their voice goes out into all the earth,*
*Their words to the ends of the world.*
[Psalm 19:1-4]

Mary's church neighbors would have been horrified if someone had desecrated several crates of Bibles. Those books are the Word of God. But the woodland that succumbed to the bulldozer's blade and the stream that no longer flows—God was speaking there, too.

But let's be fair. Almost every church I know has a parking lot. And you can't build a parking lot without the removal of trees and soil, and without causing the deaths of many of God's creatures. We need some kind of balance. As with every other human activity, we need to balance use of creation against creation's vital role in reaching those who don't yet know the Creator. In this case, I fear that the message of the gospel has not been enhanced.

We have a dilemma. Living rightly in a sacred temple when our survival seems to require damaging it in some way looks like it could be a complicated business. How can we see creation as part of God's choir and still live in it, knowing that whatever we do will have an impact? God did not leave us struggling alone with an impossible dilemma. He came to us, and showed us how we can live here as we will in heaven. He gave us a model—Jesus Christ, Son of God and Savior.

# three

## THE DIVINE CONSUMER

In middle-school and early high school, one of my children went through a serious "I have a crush" phase. Her idol was a singer with a popular contemporary Christian music group. An enormous poster hung over her bed, and every song he released was purchased, listened to, memorized and sung—over and over and over. One year the group was scheduled to sing in Chicago, just three or four hours from Madison. And it happened that the concert was close enough to my daughter's birthday that we could make her birthday party be a trip to see her idol on stage. So we bought the tickets. We even paid a bit extra so that she and her friends could stand in line before the concert to meet him in person. The great day came and everything, for once, went off without a hitch. We arrived at the concert venue in good time, stood in line, got our autographs, put in the earplugs, and enjoyed the concert. It was a highlight of her young life. My ears are still ringing.

Now suppose—just suppose—that this singer came to Madison, and he heard that his Number One fan lived in our house, and decided to visit. What would have happened? There is no question that his visit would have lifted my daughter to the rafters and beyond. "Exalted" wouldn't begin to describe it. We would have been forbidden to use the chair he sat on, and there would have been no question of putting his cup or plate back into regular circulation. Everything that he touched would have been something special.

When we think of Jesus, the Son of God, coming to earth, we often think of what we might call his "humiliation". It is not a small thing for the all-powerful creator of the universe to adopt the form of a creature, but that is exactly what happened:

> *[Jesus,] being in very nature God, did not consider equality with God something to be grasped, But made himself nothing, taking the very nature of a servant, being made in human likeness. And being found in appearance as a man, he humbled himself and became obedient to death— even death on a cross.* [Philippians 2:6-8]

Something else is just as important, though. When he came down, he raised us up, and all of creation with us. He lived here, in our house. When he walked down the street and sat in the shade of a tree, his presence was honoring and exalting the dirt, the grass, the tree, the sky. And of course it did. If my daughter's idol, the singer, had actually come to our house, the effect would have been purely imaginary. Whatever fame and reputation this man has is purely ephemeral and is already fading. He is no more worthy of praise and honor than I am—or than my daughter herself. Not so with Jesus. He made the dirt, the grass, the trees and the sky. When he arrived, everything changed.

In the last chapter we saw creation as a temple—a cosmic worship space where a divine-human relationship can be pursued. In Jesus we see God himself walking the aisles of that temple, not just standing behind the altar. This is God as one of us: eating and drinking, laughing and playing, walking and talking, sleeping and working. Before we heard God say that "it was good"; now we can see God himself enjoying creation. It must be good, and it must be worth taking care of.

## The Son of the Earth at home on earth

One of Jesus' favorite names for himself is "Son of Man". The title occurs 28 times in Matthew's Gospel, and with similar frequency in the other gospels. This was not an unfamiliar phrase to Jesus' original listeners, though his use of it for himself would have certainly raised eyebrows. His fellow Jews would have thought of the phrase as used by Ezekiel and Daniel, Old Testament prophets, apocalyptic writers for whom the Son of Man was a central figure. For them it spoke of the end of time when God would bring history to an end and restore all things. But they might have also thought of Adam, the first "son of man". Adam's name comes from the Hebrew word, adamah, earth. It is a reminder that "dust you are, to dust you will return."

There is no question that Jesus intended to connect his ministry with the end-times emphasis themes that "Son of Man" evokes for Ezekiel and Daniel. But the other, more down-to-earth meaning is also part of the picture he wants us to see. James Jones, Bishop of Liverpool pulls these two themes together for us in his book, Jesus and the Earth:

> It is Jesus the Son of Man who has come down to the earth
> from heaven who holds together in himself both earthy
> things and heavenly things. The vision that is given to
> the prophet Ezekiel of God is of 'one like Adam'. This hu-
> man picture of God is painted in the very earthy colours
> of the one hewn from the earth. Ezekiel's vision has stand-
> ing at the centre of the universe the figure of God drawn
> and depicted as an earthy human being. Here is the real-
> ity: Heaven and earth are not to be two separated realms
> for ever, divided by sin and evil, for the ultimate reality is
> an undivided world where all things whether on earth or
> in heaven hold together in Jesus (see Colossians 1). He is
> central to the earthing of heaven and to the heavening of

*earth. Earth and heaven belong together ...*
[Jones 2005, 62]

The fact of Jesus coming, and his genuine earthiness, rein-
forces what we've already seen. Creation must be cared for
because God made it, because he made it as a sacred worship
space in which we could meet him, and because he himself
walked along its paths, sat under its trees and used it for worship himself.

## He came eating and drinking

Knowing that Jesus walked this earth gives us a reason to
take care of it. And watching Jesus walk on the earth helps us
understand how we can live on this earth as creatures, and that
it is okay to be a consumer of the good things God placed here.
Bishop Jones again notes that

> *... the fact is that Jesus Christ, the earthy revelation of
> God, exercises a material ministry. Jesus the Son of Man,
> like his earthy ancestor Adam, came into the world 'eat-
> ing and drinking.'* [Jones 2005, 28]

Jesus was not an ascetic. In fact, people criticized him for
just the opposite:

> *John came neither eating nor drinking, and they say, 'He
> has a demon.' The Son of Man came eating and drinking,
> and they say, "Here is a glutton and a drunkard, a friend
> of tax collectors and "sinners".* [Matthew 11:18-19]

God made the world beautiful. He made it to reflect his
nature. He made it a place in which he could—and should—be
worshiped. But he also made it tasty. The trees in the Garden
were good for food. He made it full of life, and he intended
that its fruit should be consumed by the creatures he placed

in it. In fact, he set things up so creatures would have to eat other creatures in order to live—life consumes life, and thus life gives birth to life in a perpetual cycle of death and resurrection. All of this was part of what God declared to be good. At the time of Noah, humans were given permission to eat the flesh of other creatures (Genesis 9:3) as well as plants, and there is no reason to believe that Jesus did not eat meat with the rest of his countrymen.

DeWitt says, "Use—but don't abuse—God's creation." There are stiff penalties for those who would destroy in the process of using what God has given (Revelation 11:18). But the lesson from Jesus' example is this: God made us to be consumers, and it is okay to use the fruit of God's creation. He intended that we should do so.

### A carpenter, not a gardener

So Jesus came eating and drinking. He also came working. As with other Jewish rabbis of his day, he was trained in an occupation. His father was a carpenter, and he became one, too (Mark 6:3). This means he worked with wood, one of the most common materials of the earth. He cut down trees, sawed and planed, chiseled and shaped the wood, and produced things for people. In his day a carpenter would have been more of a cabinet and tool maker than a house builder, since most people built their own homes, and therefore, he almost certainly sold what he made for a profit. This would have made him a businessman as well.

This is fascinating. When my organization works with poor farmers in Africa, we often teach that God was the First Farmer, for he planted a garden. We do this intentionally—we want farmers to understand that in tending and caring for the earth, they are engaged in a God-ordained and God-glorifying occupation. It is honorable to be a farmer, and if you are one,

I would pause here to salute you, and would certainly shake your hand if we were together in the same room.

We might expect that when God arrived on earth, if he did anything, he would have been a gardener or a farmer. He would have worked the soil, as the first Adam did. This would fit neatly into what we read in Genesis about tending and caring for the earth. But no. Jesus comes on the scene as a carpenter and a businessman. He is the closest thing to an engineer that his society had. In the process of conducting his trade, he has to use the produce of creation. Living trees have to be chopped down to give him material with which to work. Further, he is making farm implements that will include yokes to harness oxen (see Matthew 11:30) and plows for them to pull through the fields. He might have made gates for farmers to pen in their sheep or other domesticated animals. Or a table for a butcher's shop. As a carpenter, Jesus would have supported many aspects of the agricultural enterprises that sustained his community.

It would be easy to take from the lessons of the last chapter an idea that we ought to be tiptoeing through the temple of creation, taking care not to disturb any of the other creatures for fear we might disrupt their worship of their Creator. That is not possible—for we have to eat, and this and every other activity of our lives has some impact on the rest of creation. Jesus shows us that that it is not necessary. Jesus would be the first to tell us that cutting down all the trees in a forest is wrong; that fishing a lake until there are no fish left is a sin; and that a manufacturing process that results in water that poisons fish and air that causes human cancers is an obscenity and a blasphemy. But he would not tell us not to cut down any trees, or take any fish. He is Son of the Earth, remember, and he shows us by his example that it is okay for us to involve ourselves—responsibly—in using the earth to manufacture, buy and sell from each other.

It would be nice to go back to the Garden of Eden. To be able to consume the fruit of creation in the peaceful harmony God originally intended. But we can't go back. It is not possible. There are simply too many human beings on earth to allow us to "go back to nature." One or two people camping in the woods can relieve themselves behind the bushes and there are no problems. In fact, the plants in the area will probably benefit. They were designed by God to accept and recycle the waste products of animals like ourselves and benefit from them. But a permanent camping area with 50 or 100 sites better have permanent toilet facilities with a septic tank, or the results will be disastrous.

Unfortunately, you will say, the results are pretty disastrous now. It's fine to say that Jesus' example allows us to be consumers and workers and businesspeople. "Just be a responsible consumer." That is like telling an alcoholic to drink responsibly. But how can we do that? Responsible consuming is not what we see when we look at the world today. People are consuming what they don't need and not enjoying it at all. They work without satisfaction for years to pay off debts for things they bought but didn't need, while millions of others work themselves to death and barely have enough to survive from one day to the next. And the earth suffers under the burden of such consumption.

It looks like we need more than an example. We need something to fix whatever is wrong.

# four

## DIAGNOSIS: SIN

For more than 15 years my wife Susanna has suffered from a variety of physical ailments that defied analysis. We went from doctor to doctor. We researched and studied. We managed her symptoms, sometimes with medical help, sometimes without. We had some helpful and sympathetic doctors and some that, frankly, should not be practicing medicine. But we always felt like we were playing catch-up, because neither we nor our medical team could get a handle on the underlying causes. What was the disease? If we knew that, we could, perhaps, begin to make progress.

Eight years ago we changed our medical plan. Because we were moving from one HMO to another, we had to change our entire medical team. We never made a better decision in our lives. With new people looking at Susanna's history, it seemed as if overnight we had a new treatment plan, new medications, and greatly improved quality of life. How did this happen? One of our new doctors gave us something we had not had before: a diagnosis. He was able to identify the disease at the root of all of the symptoms. With that new understanding came more tools, more appropriate use of the tools we already had— and a much, much better outcome.

"A good diagnosis is half the cure." We know that from experience. And that story illustrates a major difficulty with the modern environmental crisis. In chapter one I summarized several aspects of that crisis: It's a global crisis, a population crisis, a prosperity crisis, a poverty crisis and a political crisis. But these are like Susanna's symptoms. We can look at each one, we can try to manage them—but they don't tell us what the underlying disease is, and without that diagnosis we are doomed to a series of Band-Aid efforts that never get to the root of the problem. Without a diagnosis, there is no cure, and without a cure, no hope.

### "We didn't mean to ..."

If you are a parent you've heard the crash, as a ball sails through a window, or as two children playing tag in the living room collide with the priceless lamp sent by Aunt Jane twenty-three years ago. What do you always hear next? "But Mom ... we didn't mean to ... "

That phrase echoes down the halls of human history. Jared Diamond's book, *Collapse*, is a study of a number of civilizations and societies from prehistoric times to the present that encountered difficulties—often environmental—and disappeared. A classic example is the civilization on Easter Island in the south Pacific:

> The overall picture for Easter is the most extreme example of forest destruction in the Pacific, and among the most extreme in the world: the whole forest gone, and all of its tree species extinct ...I have often asked myself, "What did the Easter Islander who cut down the last palm tree say while he was doing it?" [Diamond 2005, 107]

I suspect he would have said what the children said about Aunt Jane's lamp: "We didn't mean to!" Have you read Dr.

Seuss' book, "The Lorax"? It is now more than 30 years old—
but it's worth reading again. The Once-ler, a business-type
creature, faces off against the Lorax. Once-ler discovers Truf-
fula trees and proceeds to chop them down to make Thneeds—
useless things that "everyone needs." The Lorax "speaks for
the trees, which you seem to be chopping as fast as you please."

Even if you haven't read the book you can guess where the
story goes: The last tree is chopped down, and Once-ler is left
amid crumbling factories beneath a smelly sky to wonder why
and how all this happened:

> *I meant no harm. I most truly did not.*
> *But I had to grow bigger. So bigger I got.*
> *I biggered my factory. I biggered my roads.*
> *I biggered my wagons. I biggered the loads*
> *of the Thneeds I shipped out. I was shipping them forth*
> *to the South! To the East! To the West! To the North!*
> *I went right on biggering...selling more Thneeds.*
> *And I biggered my money, which everyone needs.*

"I meant no harm." "We didn't mean to." No one does. But
we can't seem to stop ourselves. Why?

### Consumerism is a spiritual problem

Dr. Seuss was communicating—in a way only he could—a
concern about materialism and consumerism. Dave Roberts, a
writer for online Grist Magazine, recently addressed the same
issues in a contemporary context:

> *What's striking about the "frenzied grasping for stuff"*
> *is not the stuff but the frenzied grasping. We seem per-*
> *petually unfulfilled, convinced that just a slightly big-*
> *ger house or faster car or more flattering pair of jeans or*
> *higher-capacity mp3 player will fill the holes inside us.*

*I don't write this off to simple greed. And though there is an advertising industry devoted to stoking and exacerbating these feelings, I don't think it could create them from whole cloth.* **Why the perpetual, gnawing sense of dissatisfaction?**
[Grist Blog, 2005; emphasis mine]

Several years earlier, John DeGraaf, PBS and KCTS Television (Seattle) produced a television program and book called *Affluenza*. Here is John's definition of the term that he created:

**affluenza**, *n. 1. The bloated, sluggish and unfulfilled feeling that results from efforts to keep up with the Joneses. 2. An epidemic of stress, overwork, waste and indebtedness caused by dogged pursuit of the American Dream. 3. An unsustainable addiction to economic growth.*
[affluenza.org]

These are not Christian commentators, but they come close to an accurate diagnosis. Dave Roberts in particular is asking the right question: "Why the perpetual, gnawing sense of dissatisfaction?"

I can answer Dave with one word, but it needs some explanation. The word is "Sin", but I'm not using it as most people might. Most of us will think that "sin"is something that someone does. Murderers sin. Bank robbers sin. Politicians who lie sin. The kid running into Aunt Jane's lamp sinned—maybe (he deserves his day in court—it might have been his sister chasing him ... ). But when I buy a new mp3 player or a new car? How is that a sin?

Clearly there's a bit more to this concept of sin. Let's take a short detour back to the beginning of the story, to the Garden of Eden.

## Relationships falling like dominoes

"God's original plan was to hang out in a garden with a bunch of naked vegetarians." So says the bumper sticker on one of our cars. And that pretty much explains how things started. Adam and Eve in the Garden, naked and happy. Eat anything you want, sleep in the sun, name some animals if you get bored. Only one tiny prohibition: Don't touch the tree in the middle of the Garden. Of course, the serpent comes along, "Try it—you'll like it." They listened, they ate—and the rest is history.

Let's look at the scene for a minute. There were Adam and Eve, fruit juice still on their chins. They "heard the sound of the Lord God as he was walking in the Garden in the cool of the day, and they hid from the Lord God ..." [Genesis 3:8] They heard the sound of God in the Garden; what I hear is the sound of relationships shattering. Like dominoes, they fall one after another:

a) *Their relationship with God was broken.* Implicit in their relationship with God was his right to command them, and their obligation to obey. Having dispensed with their side of the arrangement, they could not face him, and so they hid. Separation. Alienation. Because they were created to live with—and within—God, disruption of this primary relationship led immediately to inner turmoil.

b) *Their relationship with themselves was broken.* Adam says to God, "I was afraid because I was naked ..." [Genesis 3:10] Pages have been written on this short phrase. It could mean many things; at the very least, it shows that people who had been at peace with themselves are now filled with guilt and shame. There's an inner turmoil evident here that was absent before Adam disobeyed. And because each of these sinners could not live with themselves, they could not live with each other.

c) *Their relationship with each other was broken.* It doesn't take long for the first marital argument to break out: "The woman you put here with me—she gave me some fruit from the tree, and I ate it." [Genesis 3:12] Whether the discord is between spouses, parents and children, neighbors on the street or heads of state about to go to war, it all started here. Shattered community. Being unable to live with each other, it is not surprising that they were no longer able to live in harmony with other members of God's creation.

d) *Their relationship with the rest of creation was broken.* God pronounces his curse on the serpent, on the woman and on the man. In pronouncing judgment on Adam, God says,

> *Cursed is the ground because of you;*
> *through painful toil you will eat of it all the days of your*
>    *life.*
> *It will produce thorns and thistles for you,*
> *and you will eat the plants of the field.*
> *By the sweat of your brow you will eat your food,*
> *until you return to the ground, since from it you were*
>    *taken;*
> *For dust you are, and to dust you will return.*
> [Genesis 3:17-19]

This is presented as a criminal judgment, but Adam's doom is also the logical outcome of what has gone before. He was created by God to live in harmony with the rest of creation. That harmony depended on an ongoing relationship with the Creator. He broke that relationship, and disharmony—disease, thorns, thistles—follows as surely as night follows day.

### *Sin as Sinfulness*

Adam and Eve's disobedience, breaking their relationship with God, created a new condition we can call *sinfulness*. This is sin-as-something-one-is as opposed to sin-as-something-one-does. Adam and Eve started us down this path. Sinfulness makes us unfulfilled and dissatisfied because we don't have God. It drives us to selfishness and greed. It's creates in us a compulsion to find satisfaction and meaning anywhere we can. Sinfulness is the virus that carries the affluenza disease John

DeGraaf identified, that infects us with Dave Robert's "perpetual, gnawing sense of dissatisfaction", that fills shopping malls with people who already own more than they can use, and owe more than they can pay off. The consumer-driven lifestyle is a symptom of sin. So is the poisoned air that comes from a factory whose owners have neglected to install appropriate filters. And so is war of every kind, with the loss of life to humans and the devastation of God's creation that inevitably results.

Let's get back to your mp3 player. Buying it is not necessarily a sin. But it might be. If you are buying it for your brother who is about to ship out for an overseas tour of duty, no, it's not a sin. If you're getting it because it's newer and bigger and better than your old one, or you just don't know why you're buying it but it might make you forget that fight with your boyfriend and its either an mp3 player or that new top that you saw over at Macy's—if that is the case, then yes, it's a sin.

We begin to understand why the environmental crisis is proving to be such a tough problem to solve. The stress we put on God's creation is caused in large part by our sinfulness as well as our sins. It is what we are that drives us to do what we do. Technological solutions will not solve a problem that originates in the human heart. Nor will government policies. We need changes in behavior. We need transformed lives. For it turns out that sin is far more than an academic question. Sin has consequences.

### The wages of (environmental) sin

It was an historic evening in our house. Our son had just received his driver's license, and was driving his sister to their youth group meeting for the first time. After giving all of the usual parental admonitions, we set a nine pm curfew. I knew what to expect. Sure enough, nine o'clock came and there was no car in the driveway. 9:01. 9:02. At 9:03, we heard car doors slam, and steps on the front sidewalk. An infraction of three minutes was hardly serious, but if you had been there you might have thought my children had been an hour late. I threw the book at them. Why did I do that? I wasn't angry—to be honest I would have been a little surprised if they had come back on time that first night. No, I wanted to communicate a very important principle to a young man (and his sister) about to enter a world of high speed and great danger: Rules matter.

As a family, we attempted to have firm but reasonable rules, and we often debated and sometimes modified those rules as children got older. If you ask our older children, you will hear that we modified them far too much for the younger ones, which seems to be a universal tendency as parents get older, wiser and maybe just plain tired. There is no question that sometimes we were too strict—and other times, possibly too lenient. However, the guiding principle never changed. The rules had to be obeyed. Sin has consequences . . .

This is a fundamental principle in the Bible and in life. God created us to live in harmony with him, and in a comfortable web of relationships within his creation. Any break in those relationships—sin—results in consequences. "The wages of sin is death" (Romans 3:23) is a phrase known to every evangelical Christian, and here it means eternal, spiritual death. Apart from God's grace, sin leads to eternal punishment.

We don't always have to wait until death to see the consequences of sin. Sins that affect our bodies (smoking, drugs, overeating) often result in pain and suffering now. And sometimes there is a clear connection between abuse of God's creation and disastrous consequences that follow:

> *Woe to you who add house to house and join field to field*
> *till no space is left and you live alone in the land.*
> *The LORD Almighty has declared in my hearing:*
> *"Surely the great houses will become desolate,*

*the fine mansions left without occupants.*
*A ten-acre vineyard will produce only a bath (six gallons)*
*of wine,*
*a homer (six bushels) of seed only an ephah (about half a*
*bushel) of grain.*
[Isaiah 5:8-10]

The prophet Isaiah is using the language of spiritual judgment to describe what we can recognize as the ecological consequences of overcrowding and overworking of agricultural land. Call it a 'judgment' or an 'environmental consequence'. It does not matter which term we use. Rules matter. Sin has consequences. Environmental problems are sin problems.

What we are seeing in the world today is ample evidence that rules matter. We cannot disobey with impunity. There are limits to how far we can push our rebellion against God when it comes to his creation. After too much abuse, the land will refuse to produce crops. The ocean will stop yielding fish. Wells will dry up. Rules matter. Sin has consequences. My son wasn't happy when I called him on his three minute infraction. But he never violated a curfew again. He learned that rules do matter, but that within the rules there could be peace and freedom. If he was going to be late, he learned to call. He explained, we negotiated. He learned to live within the rules. But getting back inside God's rules is not so simple. Who do we call to say we're late and we're lost? It is good and necessary to learn what the rules are—that is the role of ecology and biology. And it is fine to say that God's rules for living in his creation are good, and that we need to get back inside that web of relationship. But we can't. The web has been broken.

# REVERSING THE CURSE

It is March, 2006. I am looking at more than 260 pastors and denominational leaders from all over East Africa. We are near the end of a four day conference on "God and Creation". These men and women have come together to discuss and learn about the issues related to the environmental crisis as it affects Kenya and East Africa. As we meet, Kenya is experiencing one of the worst droughts in its modern history; causes, consequences and remedies for environmental abuse are on everyone's mind. We have had plenty of practical workshops on farming and irrigation. Participants have learned about tree planting and water harvesting. But this has not been a typical environmental conference. Most of our time has been spent in worship and Bible study. Now, in the final session, I am holding a document that I am about to ask every participant to read together and then to sign. But first I ask for prayer. And the prayers begin to pour out. In English. Kiswahili. Kikuyu. And in other tribal languages. I understand none of these, but I know that they are prayers of thanksgiving to God for his grace and love. Prayers of confession for sinning against him in how we have treated our land. Prayers for help as we seek to learn to manage our farms in ways that will bring glory to his name.

And then, with a delightful mix of African, European and American accents, we read our covenant together.

> *We believe in one God, the Creator, Owner and Sustainer of all things*
> *... We believe God calls us to be stewards of His Creation*
> *... We believe the environmental crisis emerging in East Africa poses a critical threat to our future*
> *... We confess that the Church has responded poorly to this issue*
> [ Mobilizing God's People—Appendix I]

If you had been visiting from another environmental organization, you probably would have been confused. What does this religiosity have to do with the environment? We have a practical crisis on our hands. Surely what is needed is trees— training—regulations—planning—funding. But prayer? What does prayer have to do with anything?

### Reconciliation before Restoration

We have established that the cause of the environmental crisis is our sinfulness: It's a spiritual problem, and we have to have a solution that addresses that problem. It's no good trying to dress up the same old solutions with new language. If it's a "spiritual" problem, it has to have a "spiritual" solution.

This is what Paul is talking about in Colossians 1, a key passage we cannot avoid coming back to over and over:

> *For God was pleased to have all his fullness dwell in him [Jesus] ...and through him to reconcile to himself all things, whether things on earth or things in heaven, by making peace through his blood, shed on the cross.*
> [Colossians 1:19-20]

If the problem is alienation (read, separation), the solution is reconciliation. The central message of the Bible is that God ac-

complished reconciliation—we also use the term redemption—
through Jesus' death on the cross. All of us who call ourselves
Christians or Christ-followers are in agreement on this point.

But what does it mean for God to "reconcile to himself all
things?" The portion I quoted above is part of a longer paragraph in which the exact phrase occurs five times, and similar
wording four more times, for a total of nine occurrences in one
short paragraph:

> *He is the image of the invisible God, the firstborn over
> all creation. For by him all things were created: things
> in heaven and on earth, visible and invisible, whether
> thrones or powers or rulers or authorities; all things were
> created by him and for him. He is before all things, and
> in him all things hold together. And he is the head of
> the body, the Church; he is the beginning and the first-
> born from among the dead, so that in everything he might
> have the supremacy. For God was pleased to have all his
> fullness dwell in him, and through him to reconcile to
> himself all things, whether things on earth or things in
> heaven, by making peace through his blood shed on the
> cross.* [Colossians 1:15-20]

The "all things" that were created are the "all things" that
are being held together, and the "all things" that are being rec-
onciled through the blood of Jesus.

There is a worship song we occasionally sing with a line that
goes something like, "he (God) thought of me alone' It's a nice
idea, but nothing could be further from the truth. What God
thought of when he sent his Son to die on the cross was not "me
alone" or "you alone"—it was nothing less than creation-wide
redemption. It was a plan that would reach to every corner of
the universe and that would reclaim every square inch damaged by our sin. The implications for the environmental crisis
are obvious—creation damaged by our sin can be restored by
our redemption.

But that's a bit of a leap. How does it happen?

*Putting the dominoes back in place*

Like many kids, young and old, I used to enjoy playing with dominoes. Not playing the game, you understand, but playing with the tiles. Setting them up in long chains, and when all was ready, carefully knocking the first one over. If all went according to plan, each domino would knock the next one in the line, and one by one, all would fall over. In the last chapter, we used that image to describe the series of relationships shattered by Adam and Eve's disobedience. As we think of how they are restored by redemption through Jesus, the same domino imagery is useful again. As the domino tiles fall, each pushes on the next, and eventually all are lying flat. But if you want to pick them up, you have to start with the first one that fell over, not with the last one. They have to be set up in the order in which they fell. The same is true as we begin to restore relationships broken by sin.

Just as each broken relationship caused the next one to break, so each restored relationship makes possible the restoration of the next. Here's what I mean:

a) *We begin with our relationship with God being restored.* Theologians call this "regeneration". You may refer to it as "personal salvation". It's what happens when each one of us, becoming aware of our sins and our sinfulness (see Chapter 5), come to God asking for forgiveness and accepting his gift of grace and forgiveness. Peace with God makes it possible now to experience inner peace as well.

b) *Our relationship to ourselves is restored.* Adam and Eve revealed inner turmoil when they became aware that they were naked. You and I experience a combination of guilt, shame, anxiety, discouragement and despair. It doesn't happen right away, but an important part of the Christian experience is the gift of inner peace as, having accepted God's forgiveness, we can be at peace with ourselves. Trusting him we can release anxiety about the future. Knowing him we have purpose for living.

The agent of this healing process is the Holy Spirit, and theologically we call it "sanctification". People at peace with themselves find it possible to live peacefully with each other.

c) *Our relationship with other people is restored.* Sin and inner turmoil lead to family and community conflict; redemption and inner peace are the foundation on which we can build a network of authentic relationships, in marriages, in families, and with people all around us—church, work, school. The Bible's word for God-centered community is "koinonia", and it is the basis for the institution we call the Church. We're going to have a lot more to say about the Church in the next chapter. Learning to live together in peaceful and happy social networks becomes a foundation for restoring our relationship with nature and the created order.

d) Finally, *our relationship with the rest of creation is restored.*

Or it should be.

I expect you will agree with me that the restoration of the first three relationships is a natural and expected result of God's redemption. Relationships restored are an indication that a person is a follower of Jesus. You can tell by looking at their lives. People who have their sins forgiven should experience inner peace and joy. They should have marriages and families and community relationships that exhibit the grace and peace of God.

Conversely, lack of progress in any of these relationships is a spiritual warning sign. For example, Peter tells husbands to treat their wives well, "so that nothing will hinder your prayers" (I Peter 3:7). There is a direct correlation between a husband's relationship with God, as measured in the effectiveness of his prayers here, and how he treats his wife. The same is true of parents and children.

But my relationship to creation? Do I really want to go there? The same logic would mean that how I treat my dog and how I treat my lawn and how I dispose of batteries is a measure of my faith. This is a leap few of us have taken, but it seems hard to avoid:

If our relationship with creation is broken because of sin (and it is),

> *Cursed is the ground because of you; through painful toil you will eat of it all the days of your life. It will produce thorns and thistles for you ...* [Genesis 3:17]

and if the redemption that brought us salvation was intended to restore that relationship (and it is),

> *For God was pleased to have all his fullness dwell in him, and through him to reconcile to himself all things, whether things on earth or things in heaven, by making peace through his blood, shed on the cross.*
> [Colossians 1:19-20]

and if non-human creation is waiting with anticipation for that relationship to be restored (and it is),

> *The creation waits in eager expectation for the sons of God to be revealed. For the creation was subjected to frustration, not by its own choice, but by the will of the one who subjected it, in hope that the creation itself will be liberated from its bondage to decay and brought into the glorious freedom of the children of God. We know that the whole creation has been groaning as in the pains of childbirth right up to the present time.*
> [Romans 8:19-22]

then the conclusion is unavoidable. Our relationship to creation is part of the same process as all of the others. And just as with the other relationships, a positive relationship here is a sign of spiritual growth and maturity—and a poor or negative relationship is a warning sign of problems. In fact, how I treat my dog and my lawn and how I dispose of my waste really is a measure of how well God's redemption is working in my life.

## A peace that passes understanding

There is a Hebrew word that describes the fulfillment of restored relationships that God's reconciliation is seeking to accomplish: Shalom. In its simplest definition it means "Peace", and is, to this day, in daily use throughout the Middle East as part of the most common greeting. Hebrew, Arabic, Persian, Urdu and several other languages all use some variant of this word. I grew up with "Salaam aleikum—Waleikum Salaam" in my brain: "Peace to you—And to you also, Peace."

The "Peace" of *shalom* is much more than lack of conflict. Think of a quiet evening marked by calm, stillness, and tranquility. The noise of the highway is dying away, the sun is setting, and the ducks quack quietly down on the pond. Overhead, stars begin to appear one by one. It's a peaceful setting, and there is a feeling of rest and completeness. Now we are beginning to catch a glimpse of what God means when he holds out *shalom* as a goal and a promise:

> *The LORD bless you and keep you;*
> *the LORD make his face shine upon you*
> *and be gracious to you;*
> *the LORD turn his face toward you*
> *and give you peace.*
> [Numbers 6:24-26]

*Shalom* is complete restoration: the curse reversed and all of the dominoes set back up, God's original web of relationships intact, and human beings fulfilling our role as God's choirmasters, living out our lives in obedience and worship and all of creation around us to sing his praises. That is full redemption!

*Rejoining the celestial orchestra*

Let me share a story that helps me to grasp what redemption and reconciliation means.

I was waiting on the high school gym bleachers, squeezed in with hundreds of other parents, while the gymnasium floor slowly filled with more than 900 young people. Each one held a violin, viola or other instrument in one hand, a bow in the other. The Madison, Wisconsin Annual All City Strings Festival was about to begin.

I was astounded when we moved to Madison to discover a wonderful program simply called "Elementary Strings." Beginning in fourth grade, every child who wanted to could receive instruction in how to play a stringed instrument. Though the numbers dropped in the older grades, as many as fifty per cent of fourth graders were taking part in the program at one time. The program culminates each year with a spring "Strings Festival". After weeks of memorization and practice (no sheet music allowed) students from all of the Elementary and Middle Schools came together to form one giant orchestra on a Saturday morning. This was that Saturday.

The conductor raised his baton. 900 bows came to attention. And we were enveloped in powerful waves of beautiful, harmonious music. It was powerful. It was beautiful. And it really was music. It was unbelievable.

It reminded me of how God's redemption works out in the context of his creation. God is the celestial conductor. Actually, he's more than that. He's the instrument maker, he's the composer—and he's the audience as well. (Remember Colossians 1: "all things were created by him and for him") We human beings are key players in this celestial orchestra so we're like the violins. Each of us has an instrument, made for us by God. We have a score—his revealed will to us. Successful music depends on each one of us doing our part: We have to learn to play, and we have to keep our instruments in tune. We have to keep our eyes on the conductor, and of course, we have to follow the score. But God participates in the process from beginning to end: He gave each one of us instruments to play. He has taught us, given us the score and day by day stands at our side, pointing out parts we need to work on. He works with us to keep us in tune, and in time with his heavenly music.

It's a wonderful picture—and two things we have already talked about jump out:

When we sin by doing wrong things, it is as if we are playing the wrong notes. But our sinfulness is like having broken instruments. *Even if the notes are right, the music will be wrong.* This is why no amount of trying to "be good" will ever be good enough. In redemption God has fixed our instruments, tuned them to his note again, and given us the right music to play.

An orchestra requires a lot of musicians. We are not the only instruments playing in this orchestra. You can think of us as the violins: There are a lot of us, and God has given us the melody line. But there are also flutes and clarinets and trumpets and tubas and bass drums and kettle drums and cymbals. Every other creature—and even the inanimate members of creation— is a part of God's choir, is playing in his celestial orchestra. And further, there are no solo parts. We have to practice on our own, but the real music is played with other people—lots of other people. That is the role of the Church.

# SIX

# AMBASSADORS OF REDEMPTION

Madison, Wisconsin, my home town, is an interesting place to live. It's a great small city and I love it here—even in January, when the wind chill is hovering around 40 below. We are regularly awarded "Best Place for..." awards by national magazines. In 1996 Money Magazine thought we were the best place to live in America. In 1997, Ladies Home Journal decided we were the #1 Best City for Women; the same year, we were the third best place to raise a family, according to Parenting Magazine.

If you are college student, though, you know about Madison for some other reasons. In 2005 *Sports Illustrated* declared the University of Wisconsin-Madison the #1 Party School in the country. You may be familiar with our annual State Street riots on Halloween—you certainly are if you go to school in Minnesota, home to many of our most recent arrestees. Less well known is a spring rite known as the Mifflin Street Block Party. This is an event that involves hundreds, if not thousands of people, most of the city police force, and thousands of dollars in clean up and related costs. It has history behind it, and appears to stretch back, without a break, to the Vietnam protests of 1969. (We may be the only community in the country still protesting the Vietnam War.) The first Mifflin Street Block Party began as a dance and ended in a riot that lasted three days. And here's a local secret for you: Part of Madison's ambivalence toward events like this probably comes from the fact that many of the adults living in Madison today, including those in City Hall and the State Capitol were students who participated in those early "celebrations."

The annual lead up to "The Block Party" is boringly familiar. As the date approaches, we see stories in the paper cautioning about the dangers of drinking. The University paper rehearses the history and debates the city's latest proposals to curb violence and protect the partiers from themselves. This year there will be new strategies and more severe penalties to enforce the rule of law. (We read the same stories last year.) There are letters in the paper pleading for the party to be shut down: Our community doesn't need this. (We read the same letters last year, too.) In the end, the party will come. Chaos will reign for a night. Some will be arrested, more than last year or less. Some will be hospitalized. Someone may even die. And in the morning there will be—disaster. Garbage from one end of the street to the other. Partiers will rouse themselves, look at the wreck of the street, and possibly the wreck of their lives, and wonder, Was it worth it? Eventually city crews will show up. The street will fade back to normal. Life will go on. . .

That's the way it has been every year since The Party started. But in 2005 something different happened. That year several people from Blackhawk Church got a crazy idea. "Let's serve our community by cleaning up after the Block Party." Word went out by email and text message, and at six on Sunday, more than 50 people, rubber gloves and trash bags in hand, formed a line and began marching down Mifflin Street. In front of them, a carpet of bottles, cans, paper trash and worse. Behind them, the street was clean. By midmorning, the job was done—but the repercussions were just beginning. Television crews showed up at church. No one at church called them. The goal was not publicity. But they came because they could not understand what had happened. Why would Christians—opposed to everything that "The Party" represents—come out at six in the morning and do the clean up? The answer was simple: "We wanted to show what it means to love your neighbor."

This is true Christianity. This is the Church at work in the world. When this kind of thing happens, the world notices. It can't help it.

## Let the church be the Church

This story *was* newsworthy. Who expected a church to do something like that? But it should not have been newsworthy to those of us 'inside' the church. Here is an example of a church doing exactly what it was created by God to do. As that line of people formed early on that Sunday morning, they were demonstrating the redemption-reconciliation pattern that we have been describing throughout this book: Individuals whose relationship with God had been restored by forgiveness from God (the first relationship) and who were therefore at peace with themselves (the second relationship) joined hands with other people to work together (the third relationship) to clean up a mess in the world (the fourth relationship). The Mifflin Street Block Party clean up shows what happens when God's redemptive plan hits the street.

Unfortunately, this kind of initiative is newsworthy because it is all too rare. In fact, if we look beyond alcoholic bacchanals to other more common ways in which humanity harms creation, the church is as often to be found among those partying rather than among those trying to clean up the mess. Wendell Berry wrestles with this issue as he considers the effect religion and religious people have had on his own corner of creation through the years:

*Such religion as has been openly practiced in this part of the world has promoted and fed upon a destructive schism between body and soul, Heaven and earth. It has encouraged people to believe that the world is of no importance, and that their only obligation is to submit to certain churchly formulas in order to get to Heaven. **And so the people who might have been expected to care most selflessly for the world have had their minds turned elsewhere**—to a pursuit of "salvation that was really only another form of gluttony and self-love, the desire to perpetuate their lives beyond the life of the world. The Heaven-bent have abused the earth thoughtlessly, by inattention, and their negligence has permitted and encouraged others to abuse it deliberately.* [Berry 2002, 22; emphasis mine]

Berry's analysis is perfectly sound. But he is describing a Christian experience that sees redemption as applying only to the first or second set of relationships, and sometimes to the third. If we can extend our view of redemption to cover all that God intends it to cover—all four relationships restored—Berry's complaint goes away, heaven and earth draw together, and *shalom* becomes more reality than dream.

But we need to get hold of a definition. "Church" can mean so many things that discussion easily becomes confusing or meaningless. Please do note that my purpose here is to keep things relatively simple and practical. I could give you a theologically complex definition with all the appropriate shadings of meaning, footnotes and historical discussions. That would be more precise but less useful. Allow me, then, to hide behind the useful caveat, "for purposes of this discussion".

For purposes of this discussion, *Church* does not mean a building or a denomination. The former never occurs biblically, and the latter is a construct convenient for modern organizational purposes that does not have a great deal of application to our discussion here. As I am using the term, there are two interlocking dimensions: Taking a wide-angle view, the *Church* (uppercase C) means the whole Christian "movement" or some aspect of it—all of Jesus' followers, moving together, often in fits and starts, but still living the plan of redemption and reconciliation we described in the last chapter. This *Church* might be the worldwide Christian community, all Christians in a particular geographical area (the Church in Madison, the Church in Kenya) or the entire movement through history, from the time of Jesus to his future return. Changing to a close up lens, *church* (lowercase c) means a group of people who have joined together to follow Jesus' teachings, to worship together and to be a community.

To try to avoid confusion, I have tried to be consistent in using *Church* and *church* appropriately to distinguish these two ways of thinking, though inevitably the meanings will overlap from time to time, for these two dimensions fit together, and really can't be separated. The church is always a local fellowship—ordinary people trying to find God's will in their lives and in their community and learning to live and to honor him by loving each other day by day and week by week. But this fellowship, or these fellowships, for there are millions of them, always move in an atmosphere that connects them to each other and to those that have gone before and those that will follow. The union is almost mystical.

When the *church* connects with the *Church*, amazing things can and do happen. "Think globally; Act locally" describes nothing so much as it describes the Church of Jesus Christ being and doing what Jesus has created it to do.

### I will build my Church

And what he has created it to do is to be the embodiment and fulfillment of his redemption/reconciliation plan on earth. For the church/Church is the creation of Jesus Christ himself.

He anticipated it when he said to Peter:

*. . . I will build my Church and the gates of Hades will not overcome it.* [Matthew 16:18]

He commissioned his disciples to build it:

*All authority in heaven and on earth has been given to me. Therefore, go and make disciples of all nations.* [Matthew 28:18-19]

And the final consummation of earthly human history is presented as the marriage of Christ and his Church:

*Then I heard what sounded like a great multitude, like the roar of rushing waters and like loud peals of thunder, shouting: "Hallelujah! For our Lord God Almighty reigns. Let us rejoice and be glad and give him glory! For the wedding of the Lamb has come, and his bride has made herself ready.* [Revelation 19:6-7]

This is significant because the person who established the Church and called it to a ministry of reconciliation is the same one who created the cosmos, who holds it together and who died to redeem it and to reconcile it to himself. There is a glorious symmetry to God's plan that we discovered in that Colossians passage we keep coming back to. Look at it again—buried in the middle are these words:

*. . . all things were created by him and for him. He is before all things, and in him all things hold together. **And he is the head of the body, the Church**; he is the beginning and the firstborn from among the dead, so that in everything he might have the supremacy.* [Colossians 1:16-18]

The One who is before all things, who made all things, who holds all things together, and who shed his blood on the cross to reconcile all things to himself is the head of his body the

Church. The center of God's redemptive plan rests on two things: Jesus' sacrificial death on the cross which activates it, and the formation of the Church, which implements it. In II Corinthians Paul makes this role even more explicit:

> *All this is from God, who reconciled us to himself through Christ and gave us the ministry of reconciliation: that God was reconciling the world to himself in Christ, not counting men's sins against them. And he has committed to us the message of reconciliation. We are therefore Christ's ambassadors, as though God were making his appeal through us. We implore you on Christ's behalf: Be reconciled to God!* [II Corinthians 5:18-20]

The redemption, reconciliation and restoration that God is accomplishing in the world is being accomplished through the Church. Cleaning up Mifflin Street and activities like it should not be occasional, newsworthy add-ons to a church's program. They should *be* the church's program—as closely tied to the church's reason for being as performing baptisms or celebrating communion.

### Far as the curse is found

I've been around the block a few times with local churches. I have been a pastor. A deacon. An elder. A youth group leader. A Sunday school teacher. A janitor. I know how to make church coffee. I know the church as well as anyone—and I know how far the *best* church falls from any kind of biblical ideal. There are times when I am quite sure that I or anyone could have come up with a better plan than this one.

So why did God go to all this trouble? What was he thinking? Reading the mind of God is presumptuous at best, but even so, it appears to me that God's plan of reconciliation seems to rest on redemption taking place in the same arena where the curse has reigned supreme—that is, in this physical creation. Its part of that symmetry we referred to above. Isaac Watts put the idea into one of our favorite Christmas carols:

> *No more let sins and sorrows grow,*
> *Nor thorns infest the ground;*
> *He comes to make His blessings flow*
> **Far as the curse is found...**
> [Isaac Watts, *Joy to the World*]

In God's wisdom, he seems to have decided that the creatures that caused the curse in the first place—you and me, the human race—should be those charged with the job of reversing its effects. Unable to earn our salvation or in any way make ourselves right or righteous before God, he nonetheless has offered us a ministry of reconciliation—an opportunity to help set right what we caused to go wrong.

You may have had the kind of experience I had recently. Knowing I would shortly be between jobs, an acquaintance invited me to an evening sales demonstration for a multi-level marketing company. We were treated to a review of some very good products—the company makes good stuff—and we were encouraged to sign on as sales representatives; we could earn a good commission on each sale to our friends, neighbors or ourselves. But then the presentation got interesting. The secret to success, we were told, was to recruit more people to sell under us. We would get credit for all of their sales. And when they recruited more people under them, we would get credit for those sales, too. Eventually, hundreds of people would be selling, and we could sit back and just rake in the money. This is called multi-level marketing. There are products to sell, but the real goal is to sell memberships.

Outsiders could be forgiven for confusing some evangelical churches with multilevel marketing organizations. It sometimes seems like our mission is to make disciples who will make disciples who will make disciples—until the end comes and

Jesus returns to take us all to be with him for ever and ever, Amen. This is plainly not the case. We ought to reach all nations and see that every person on earth hears the good news of Jesus Christ. Yes! But this is not the end of our mission. It is only the beginning.

So how do we get the mission of the Church out to Mifflin Street and beyond? Specifically, how can a group of people that might know how to conduct a prayer meeting but doesn't know anything about water quality make a difference? Let's get practical.

### A values-based organization

One of Wendell Berry's phrases that we quoted above sticks in my mind: "the people who might have been expected to care most selflessly for the world have had their minds turned elsewhere." [Berry 2002, 23] Everyone who wrestles with the problem of Christians and the environment starts at the same point: "These people *should care* more than anyone else." Berry's complaint is a pointer to truth: The church has been expected to care, and should care about these things more than other people because of *what she already believes.*

My own experience is instructive. My shift in career toward environmental stewardship forced me into a period of intensive self-examination. This had not been part of my thinking. But I discovered something that surprised me. I was already an environmentalist. I just didn't know it yet. I already believed God made the world. I believed that he reveals himself through his creation. I believed he put me here to do his will, and doing his will includes taking care of his creation. I had an entire theology—value system, if you prefer—that was deeply embedded with environmental or creation care principles. It was packed away in the attic, and needed to be dusted off. But it didn't take much to get it out and functioning again.

I suspect the same thing is true for you, if you are a follower of Jesus Christ. Nothing that I have presented in this book should be new to you. There is nothing here that anyone who takes the Bible seriously and who practices a Biblical faith should be able to take issue with. We Christians may have been asleep on this subject for a few years, but we don't have to stay asleep. We already believe everything we need to.

It's time for us to wake up.

## An agent for change

We concluded in chapter four that the environmental crisis is essentially a disease caused by sin and by sinfulness. Bad behavior—materialism, greed, selfishness—caused and perpetuated by a tendency toward and an inability to break out of bad behavior patterns lies at the root of the problem. Any psychologist or psychiatrist could tell us what we need to do: Break the pattern so we can stop the behavior. If this sounds like therapy, you're right. True spiritual healing is what we need. And this is something the Church is very, very good at: Helping people to understand their sin and guilt, coming to God for forgiveness and help, and changing how we live. We need to apply our ability to confront and change behavior to creation care. Environmental problems are sin problems—and sin is something the Church knows how to handle.

Will it work? Can Christians make a difference? These are early days—but the signs are promising.

In the Chesapeake Bay area, a community of local fishermen listened to a graduate student, Susan Drake (now Susan Emmerich); they became aware of the disconnect between what they said they believed in church on Sunday, and how they were actually acting when they abused the waters and shellfish beds from which they made a living. They signed a public covenant together—in church—and changed the way they lived and worked in a dramatic fashion. The entire environmental community of Maryland took notice.

In the Pennsylvania farm country, some of those same fishermen took the time to show their Christian brothers who were farmers that how they fertilized their fields was damaging the bay and hurting the shellfish beds the fishermen depended on. The farmers determined, before God, that they had to change the way they were farming. How else could they be said to be loving their neighbors? And they changed.

In Kenya and East Africa, at the conference I described earlier, 260 church leaders signed a public declaration in March, 2006, declaring that "we believe God calls us to be good stewards of his creation" and calling on all Christians in their region to "begin developing God-centered strategies to educate, disciple, and mobilize the entire Church to action." A number of churches have since started their own tree nurseries and plans are being proposed for a Kenya-wide tree planting effort every year the week after Easter. The Church in Kenya will call the nation to celebrate the resurrection by planting God's trees.

A mobilized church can make an impact.

### A spiritual organism, a human organization

I love my Bible. Not just "the Bible" as a general term, but the particular copy of the Bible that is mine. This copy is getting a bit worn. The leather is seriously frayed on the back, and my wife is starting to talk about how tattered it looks. She wants to get me a new one. She's right, of course, but I'm not quite ready to retire the one I've got. I'm much attached to this one, though I could find the same words in a nice new one. The marks on the pages, even the pages that have been torn, remind me of experiences I have had with God while reading this book.

That strange mixture of the divine and human is what the Bible is all about. On the one hand, it is a very human docu-

ment. Written by ordinary people, it was copied by hand for
centuries, and accumulated typos and spelling mistakes. Its
thousands of manuscripts and papyri have been the subject of
and have stood up under academic research and scrutiny more
intense than that given to any other document.

And yet the Bible bears the marks of God's hand as nothing
else that we possess. It faithfully records history about God's
dealings with humanity, and teaches about God in language
that surpasses any other human literature. Was there ever a
poem in any language that could surpass the last half of the
eighth chapter of Paul's letter to the Romans for eloquence and
passion? Any more universally loved and moving poem than
the twenty-third Psalm? And with all this, for millions of us
it is an almost direct connection to God. Often I start my day
with a cup of coffee and this old, tattered Bible. I read passages
that grow more familiar as the years go by, and still I discover
new truth every time. I hear the voice of God's Holy Spirit
encouraging, or prodding me or in some other way showing
me what I need to know today. I don't mark my Bible, but you
can still tell which parts have been most meaningful to me over
the fifteen years or so that this particular copy has been my
mainstay. And that's why I hesitate to give it up. It is a map
of a spiritual journey—marking times and ways that God has
stepped into my life in a very direct and personal way.

My church is like my Bible, exhibiting the same mix of divine and human. It is a human institution, existing under a
charter granted by the secular authorities of my community
and my state. It has founding and guiding documents that are
legal in character and that are not very different from those of
other nonprofit organizations. It has members who are very human, and leaders who are even more so. It struggles with prag-
matic issues like budgets and finances and organizing dozens
of volunteers and complaints from the neighbors about cars
blocking their driveways.

But my church is not just a nonprofit organization. Its human elements are all tangled up with spiritual realities. It is a divine organism as much as a human organization, and there are times when the Spirit is very real as he moves among us while we worship and sing praises together. I have no question that important actions taken by this church—like buying a new building—have been conducted through the ordinary human medium of taking a vote, but I can believe that that vote was mysteriously guided by the Holy Spirit working through the lives of the people in the room. The divine element in church life is hard to pin down—it defies analysis—but is nonetheless real for that. And I suspect you might agree with me, and you might also have laughed and cried at the strange combination of joys and frustrations that come from trying to live with the strange organism/organization that is the Church of Jesus Christ.

It is this hybrid nature of the Church that allows it to bring something to the real problems of the environmental crisis that will be found nowhere else. The Church can deliver spiritual power to practical problems. The environmental crisis is a confusing tangle of sinful individual human behaviors, sinful corporate behavior, and the ecological realities caused by too many people, too many cars, the proliferation of exotic[1] species and the global effects of climate change—and a whole lot more. It is a scientific problem, an economic problem, a political problem, a security problem, and a moral problem—and a matter of life and death for millions. But at its root, it is a spiritual problem. The Church—properly understood and functioning in the full power of God—is the only institution or organization available to the human race that can address a problem with this many dimensions. The Church is capable of addressing every issue—repentance from sin, motivation for individual action, courage and influence to change corporate behavior, and the ability to

---

[1] A note for the nonscientific: Anything 'exotic' is something—plant or animal—that has been imported from somewhere else—it doesn't belong here and is therefore usually causing problems.

recruit and mobilize millions of people from volunteers to scientists to move into creation and do everything from tree planting to weed removal.

So how do we begin?

*Part 2: The Mission*

# seven

## LIKE A MIGHTY ARMY

The words ring out bravely:

*Like a mighty army moves the Church of God*
*Brothers we are treading where the saints have trod!*

But as I look out over this small Midwestern congregation, it hardly seems like a "mighty army." We're in the heart of the American Midwest, in an old farming community. The worshipers are all of European descent. Some have been in this community and in this church for several generations; others are newer arrivals. They work farms, and in the local community college or in industry or retail in a slightly larger community west and north of their small town. They have gathered on this Sunday, as others like them have done for more than 150 years to worship, pray, learn from the words of scripture, and wrestle the issues of their individual lives and their community. When the service is over, their discussions will revolve around the fortunes of the high school sports teams, the prospect of a cold (or warm) winter, and who is going to be on duty for nursery next Sunday.

There is another fellowship, a church meeting on the slopes overlooking Nairobi, Kenya, in a building nestled among tea plantations. People, ladies in particular, are dressed "smartly" and look like brightly colored flocks of birds coming and going. There are no cars parked at this church; the local taxis that run up and down the road a short distance away belch clouds of diesel exhaust. There is trash and garbage, especially plastic bags, everywhere you look, right to the front door of the church. The tea bushes are an important source of income for everyone in this church, but they are withered and dying from a prolonged drought. However, inside the singing is loud and lively. The sermon is prolonged and enthusiastic. The worship service goes on and on and on.

The North American congregation is far wealthier than their Kenyan brothers and sisters by almost every measure, but even so, neither of these groups can be considered much of a powerhouse when we think of the challenges represented by the global environmental crisis. Hardly the "mighty army" of the hymn we were singing that Sunday.

As you read this book, you are more likely to be from a church like the Midwestern congregation that I described than the Kenyan fellowship. And based simply on numbers of congregations, you are more likely to come from a church like this than from one of the megachurches that are featured in media reports from time to time. Around the world, most Christians will be found worshiping in small groups of less than 100. So we can say that the church has the ability to address every issue related to the environmental crisis, but it's quite another matter to see this actually happening. With the eyes of faith, perhaps we can see the Church marching through history like that mighty army; when we get down to practical realities, what we actually see is churches—thousands of small groups scattered around the world. Can these entities really be the solution to the greatest crisis facing the human race?

Yes, they can. What appears to be a weakness from a human perspective is not necessarily so when God gets into the picture:

*Brothers, think of what you were when you were called. Not many of you were wise, by human standards; not many were influential; not many were of noble birth. But God chose the foolish things of the world to shame the wise; God chose the weak things of the world to shame the strong. He chose the lowly things of this world and the despised things—and the things that are not—to nullify the things that are, so that no one may boast before him.* [I Corinthians 1:26-29]

God's plans have always been countercultural and counter-intuitive. We don't need massive campaigns and buckets of money to apply the solution of redemption and reconciliation to the problems posed by the environmental crisis. What do we need?

- A worship and teaching program that gives us clear vision of and genuine passion for God's creation—we have to feed our souls.

- Effective teaching of creation care to the next generation—we have to open the eyes of our young people.

- Meaningful and practical earth-healing ministry activities in our communities—if we don't heal our own neighborhoods, who will?

- Mission outreach that integrates earth-healing ministries and creation care teaching into church planting and development programs.

We'll look at the first one below, and the others in subsequent chapters. But I can already hear the groans from the Pastor's study. "Another program? I don't think so! No time. No money. Our ministry objectives are set, our strategic agenda has been discussed. If a few people want to do this on the side, it sounds great to me, but don't expect us to drop everything else to pursue an environmental program."

I understand the problem. I've spent some time in a pastor's study myself, and I remember the steady stream of pitches by mail, email and phone for this ministry and that ministry. All are valid, and no church can do everything. Each of us, whether at the individual level or at the church fellowship level, has to try to decide what God is calling us to do, and we have to be willing to leave the rest for someone else. This would seem to suggest that some churches might want to 'do creation care' while others 'do AIDS' and still others 'do inner city outreach'. I'm going to argue that creation care is qualitatively different from other specialty ministries, and that it needs to be brought into every aspect of church programming. Here's why.

### A challenge like no other

Let's look at the negative first: *The nature and magnitude of the problem puts creation care in a category by itself.* Nothing—not even AIDS or a flu pandemic in your community carries the urgency of the environmental crisis.

Let me share a hypothetical story. Let's say that you and I have found ourselves on a ship in the middle of the ocean transporting a large number of refugees from one country to another. We're part of a Christian relief operation—crew and staff are in this for reasons of compassion and ministry, and our objective is to care for the hundreds of people on board physically and spiritually until we arrive at our destination.

The needs of the passengers are many. Besides providing daily food and sanitation, there are medical problems, and a host of children need to be entertained and educated. We are concerned that the spiritual needs of the people not be over-looked, so we provide opportunities for worship and evangelism as well. In order to accomplish all of this, we've divided our efforts: Some of us provide food and service the restrooms. Others are involved in medical clinics throughout the ship. Still others care for children, teach classes, hold chapel services or just move throughout the vessel, sharing about Jesus wherever the opportunity arises. Some take care of administration: tracking the use of supplies, scheduling use of rooms, and seeing that volunteers are used appropriately.

Our voyage proceeds, but sometimes problems appear: An outbreak of dysentery on one of the lower decks, problems with one of the kitchens, a disagreement over whether the medical people or the school people have priority for use of a particular lounge. Being sensible folks, we start holding coordination meetings every morning in the Captain's quarters to keep track of these issues and to be sure that every service and ministry area has the resources it needs.

One morning there is a new face at the coordination meeting. The Captain introduces him: "This is our Chief Engineer, and he has some news I think you need to hear." It turns out that our vessel began to take on water during the night. The situation is serious, and solving the problem will require cooperation from everyone at the table. *"Bottom line, folks? If we don't solve the problem, we can't make it to port."*

Think about how that announcement would affect the people sitting around the table. They all have jobs to do  life has to go on, even while the leak is being investigated and fixed. Food still needs to be served, illnesses still need to be treated. More than ever, people need to be ministered to spiritually. *But the problem with the ship has to be fixed or nothing else will matter.*

This is how we need to view creation care in relation to other church ministries. They all have to go on. No question about that. But if we don't take care of the ship we're on, those other ministries won't matter much. In Haiti, normal ministry of any kind is impossible due to the terrible conditions in that country; in countries like Kenya, church leaders recognize their own vulnerability. In several informal surveys that we have conducted at Care of Creation, Inc., the environmental crisis has ranked higher than the HIV/AIDS crisis in terms of the threat these leaders feel it poses for them and their people. Why? Put it like this: *HIV/AIDS affects life—but the environment is life.*

When AIDS strikes a community, many people die. When a fishery collapses or agricultural land no longer produces, everyone dies. *If the ship springs a leak, everyone goes down.*

### When creation wins, everyone wins

But there is a big positive reason for integrating creation care in the church program. *Becoming more creation-aware and more creation-caring always enhances other ministries in a church far more than it draws resources away from them.* This should not surprise us. Extending redemption to all of creation is at the heart of God's plan for the cosmos and the church. The more we do creation care, the closer we draw to our main task.

One of the standard objections to environmental initiatives in the political and business worlds has been that it costs too much to be green. Jobs will be lost. We have to choose—it's the environment or the economy  we can't have both. Business people are discovering that this is simply wrong. Ford Motor Company recently spent two billion dollars to renovate its flagship Rouge plant in Dearborn, Michigan, and much of the effort went into innovations such as the world's largest living roof (it's covered in a grass-like plant called sedum), the planting of more than 100,000 shrubs and trees and even the installation of three honey-bee hives. These efforts are making a cleaner factory for the future, they are reversing some of the damage done in the past, and they are contributing to the company's bottom line. Ford will save millions of dollars a year by going green. Companies all over the world are discovering that green business—green manufacturing and green products—is good business.

The same thing is true in your church setting. Green programming will be effective programming. Making a conscious effort to integrate creation care with worship, Christian education and youth programs, facilities management or outreach won't hurt any of these. Every program area will be richer and more meaningful for those who participate, and functional areas like facilities will give back any investment made in thousands of dollars in savings that can be used for ministry activities.

We have nothing to lose and everything to gain. As do the creatures God put in our care. When creation wins, we all do.

### Creation in the worship service

I went to church yesterday. It was a good service. The message was on prayer, and the pastor's text was from the book of Acts. There was nothing that needed to connect with God's creation. *But three out of the five songs we sang were directly related to God and creation*, and the slides used as background for the lyrics were sunsets, mountain landscapes and pictures of galaxies from the Hubble space program. Have you noticed? Creation has a tendency to sneak into worship even when we aren't looking for it. Check your own worship experience recently: Look at the power point slides, listen to the words in the hymns or praise songs. Do you see pictures of factories? Of highways and junk yards? Do we sing praise of parking lots and shopping malls? Of course not! We see pictures of sunsets and mountains, ocean beaches and starry skies. We sing of nature and creation and the greatness of the God who made it all and who made and loves us, too.

*Mobilizing the church to respond to the environmental crisis begins with worship.* Worship is at the heart of what it means to be a church. Worship is the point in our existence where human and divine connect with each other; where the cares and worries of the present lose themselves, if only briefly, in the peace and joy of eternity. The out-of-reach concept of shalom becomes an experiential reality. This happens through music and prayer that help us focus on God, and teaching and preaching that allows us to listen to him and that encourages us to bring our lives into conformity to his nature and will.

Remember: worship is also at the heart of what God had in mind when he made creation. It is a platform for relationship. A temple in which he, God, could meet with us, his creatures, accept our worship and pour his love and grace into us. What better place to start caring for God's creation than in our regular exercise of worship? It's an easy place to start. Most of the work has already been done for us.

### Singing and praying with creation

Our music, whether traditional or contemporary, is loaded with creation themes. Think about these classics:

1225: *All Creatures of our God and King* ...

1674: *Praise God, from whom all blessings flow;*
*Praise him all creatures here below...*

1715: *I sing the mighty power of God that made the mountains rise...*

1848: *All things bright and beautiful, all creatures great and small...*

1864: *For the beauty of the earth, for the glory of the skies...*

1873: *Fairest Lord Jesus, Ruler of all nature...*

1901: *This is my father's world,*
*and to my listening ears,*
*all nature sings and round me rings*
*the music of the spheres...*

1907: *Field and forest, vale and mountain,*
*flowery meadow, flashing sea*
*chanting bird and flowing fountain*
*call us to rejoice in thee...* [ Joyful, Joyful, we adore thee]

Note the dates of these hymns. Creation care is not new, but as many modern praise songs could also be noted:

*Lord of all creation, of water earth and sky...*
—Caedmons Call

*You are the Lord, the Savior of all, God of Creation we praise you*
*We sing the songs that awaken the dawn...*
—Delerious

*From the highest of heights to the depths of the sea*
*Creation's revealing your majesty*
—Chris Tomlin

*Shout to the Lord, all the earth let us sing*
*Power and majesty, praise to the King*
*Mountains bow down and the seas will roar*
*At the sound of your name*
—Darlene Zschech

Singing about God's creation is not a 'modern innovation', but rather a return to the historical roots of our faith. Creation-oriented worship upholds some of the oldest Biblical teachings we have:

*Since the creation of the world Gods invisible qualities his eternal power and divine nature  have been clearly seen, being understood from what has been made...*
[Romans 1:20]

Worship is seeking Gods face. What better place to look than in creation?  Throughout history, from David's Psalms to today's praise choruses, worshipers and those called to lead others in worship have looked to creation for inspiration—and have found it.

Creation and Worship go together naturally. Worship that leaves out creation is like a piano player using just one hand, or a choir that has dispensed with altos and tenors. You can hear the melody, but the richness is gone. Worship that consciously and deliberately incorporates creation is worship to remember, and worship that the Spirit of God will use to change people's lives.

What elements might be included in creation-inspired worship?

- *It will use creation actively in music and prayer.* On one level this is easy. The content is already there. But it is equally important to make the connection deliberately, reading scriptures about creation (Genesis 1,2, Psalm 8, 19, 104, 148, Job 38, 39, 40, Matthew 6:26ff, Romans 8, Colossians 1, are just a few) to bridge between creation songs, or transitioning from a such a song to a prayer of thanksgiving to God for his creation.

- *It will bring creation into the worship experience.* Worship spaces should make God's world visible (open the window shades); plants and flowers can bring God's beauty to our attention.

- *It will take worship outdoors on occasion.* Jesus seldom taught indoors. We see him on mountains, in lakes, walking the fields. Moving the whole church outside might be a challenge  but is it completely out of the question once a year or so?

- *It will encourage individual worship that incorporates creation.* Effective group worship should be deliberately encouraging people to worship on their own. Teaching people how to use God's creation in their worship will transform that experience, and will begin the process that results in individual behavior and attitude changes in how they live in God's creation.

## Teaching creation care

One of the things I like about our church is that we have really, really good coffee.  It is not certain that this church is growing because of the coffee—but it's possible.  The service that my wife and I attend is called the Video Café, and it caters to people like me. Sit in the gym on folding chairs and go ahead and sip your coffee during the service.  But the coffee service raises an issue: More than eight hundred cups get used and thrown away every Sunday. In a year, that makes 40,000 cups—that's a lot of waste.

Stony Brook Community Church in western Massachusetts is different.  After-church coffee is just like the fellowship hour in a thousand other churches—but there are no disposable cups.

There is a complete selection of mugs for coffee, tea or hot chocolate. Stony Brook got rid of their disposable cups and started using ceramic mugs more than five years ago after a sermon on the implications of Christian environmental stewardship for every day life. Changing how we use disposable dishes was one of the practical suggestions given, and something must have clicked. Every time I return to this church, I am pleasantly surprised. The mugs are still there.

Those mugs are an example of what can happen when creation care teaching is a part of worship. There is a mystical power when the Word of God is preached in the context of worship that is not present in a lecture hall or seminar or classroom. When people come together to meet God, when they have spent twenty or thirty or forty minutes in worship, meditation and prayer, the preaching of the Word has a power that no other kind of speech can match. Political rallies can excite. Classroom lectures can inform. But the Word of the living God, delivered by the power of the Holy Spirit in the context of genuine worship—this can change lives.

And lives need to change. At every level, environmental problems are related to the behavior of individuals. Individuals decide whether to buy a compact car or an SUV. Individuals drive home energy consumption. And individuals make strategic business decisions that impact hundreds of stores or thousands of factory workers. *Many of those individuals are in church on Sunday,* and should be getting guidance from God's Word as they face the spiritual and moral implications of the decisions they will be making. The environmental crisis will not change until people change. And that change will not happen through mailings from the Sierra Club, or a platform plank at the Democratic or even the Republican conventions. It will happen when ordinary pastors in ordinary pulpits and ordinary Sunday school teachers begin to teach about God and creation, and when they help their people see the connections be-

tween how they live and what is happening to the world God
loves.

What should we teach? How about the "full gospel" of redemption and reconciliation that we have already examined in
earlier chapters? Just as incorporating creation themes into music worship and prayer will give them a richness and a meaning
they otherwise would lack, so adding creation care themes—
implications and application—to the teaching we are already
doing will lose nothing. Instead we will gain a new level of
richness and meaning, and we will find new ways to make the
faith practical.

### Reading two books together

Can we go too far with this? Do we need to worry that an
emphasis on creation might lead to a worship of creation itself?
Of course. We're humans, and given to excess in everything we
try to do. We have yet to find a good thing we can't spoil by
having too much.

Yes, we might so emphasize the glories of creation that we
lose sight to the creator to whom it points. A healthy worship
experience will include both songs about creation and songs
about the Savior. We have two books about God—creation and
the Bible. We study the Bible with a prayer in our hearts that
God will reveal himself to us through the words we read. When
we study or meditate on some aspect of God's world, we do the
same thing. Whether we see him in a new way in Isaiah 53 or
in a spider's web or in towering thunderclouds, we rejoice in
the vision of the One who made us. When we read both books
together, it is just as if we were cross-referencing the Gospels
of Matthew and John. Between the two, a complete picture
emerges, and the danger of error is less, rather than more.

When we have been in error about God's creation it has
been because of too little time spent in that book, not too much.

# ei**g**ht

## THE NEXT GENERATION

Calvin DeWitt, Professor of Environmental Studies at the University of Wisconsin and founder of Au Sable Institute of Environmental Studies, started his career with a turtle in his backyard at the age of three:

> *I grew up right in the city of Grand Rapids, and our lot was only 40 feet wide. But we had a nice home there and my father eventually gave over pretty much all of the backyard to my backyard zoo. And he allowed me to build a special room in the basement for my tropical fish, scorpions, cockroaches, and all sorts of worm cultures that I used to feed my animals. At peak I had 39 parakeets that I was breeding. And I took detailed notes* [DeWitt, Interview published on care2.com, 10/12/2006]

Harvard biologist and author E.O. Wilson traces the beginnings of his love for creation to age eight, when his parents gave him a microscope:

> *I then found my own little world, completely wild and unconstrained, no plastic, no teacher, no books, no anything predictable. At first I did not know the names of the water-drop denizens or what they were doing. But neither did the pioneer microscopists. Like them I graduated*

*to looking at butterfly scales and other miscellaneous objects. I never thought of what I was doing in such a way, but it was pure science.* [Wilson, *The Creation*, 144]

Francis Collins, Director of the Human Genome Project, recalls that at age fourteen:

*My eyes were opened to the wonderfully exciting and powerful methods of science. Inspired by a charismatic chemistry teacher who could write the same information on the blackboard with both hands simultaneously, I discovered for the first time the intense satisfaction of the ordered nature of the universe. The fact that all matter was constructed of atoms and molecules that followed mathematical principles was an unexpected revelation, and the ability to use the tools of science to discover new things about nature struck me at once as something of which I wanted to be a part.* [Collins, *Language of God*, 14]

These three prominent men of science have taken very different paths in life. DeWitt began in a Christian home and stayed in the faith all his life. Wilson began as a Southern Baptist, but now simply says, "I no longer belong to that faith." Collins traces a journey that began in a free-thinking household and that brought him to faith while a young doctor. But they all exude a passion for God's world that is remarkable. Even Wilson, while admitting that he is a confirmed skeptic when it comes to anything having to do with God, writes almost poetically about God's world:

*Without mystery, life shrinks. The completely known is a numbing void to all active minds. Even a laboratory rat seeks the adventure of the maze. So we are drawn to the natural world, aware that it contains structure and complexity and length of history as well, at orders of magnitude greater than anything yet conceived in human imagination. Mysteries solved within it merely uncover more mysteries beyond. For the naturalist every entrance into*

*a wild environment rekindles an excitement that is child-like in spontaneity, often tinged with apprehension—in short, the way life ought to be lived, all the time.*
[Wilson, *Future of Life*, 146]

## It starts when you're young

It seems that God's book of creation opens most easily when we are young, and this shouldn't surprise us. Jesus told us that the kingdom of heaven belongs to children (Matthew 19:14) and we might expect that his creation would as well. And always there are adults—parents and teachers—helping to turn the pages of the book: Buying a microscope. Letting the back yard become a zoo. But in these stories, and in most stories like them, one seldom sees the church.

Mobilizing the church means bringing the values of creation care to the next generation. As worship is at the heart of what the church is, training or discipleship stands at the center of what the church does. *Train a child in the way he should go ...* [Proverbs 22:6] is not just for parents. A great deal of church effort and programming is centered, as it ought to be, on conveying the truths of the faith to those who will follow us. We know that we are part of something bigger than ourselves, something that was thousands of years old when we received it, and that we are responsible to faithfully pass to those who will come after: *The things you have heard me say in the presence of many witnesses entrust to reliable men who will also be qualified to teach others.* [I Timothy 2:2]

Teaching the next generation is a way of correcting our own mistakes. Our generation has neglected creation care teaching. If that weren't the case, I wouldn't be writing this page right now. Making the effort to teach early values that you and I may have learned late is not hypocrisy—its love and common sense. Of course, we may find out that they are already ahead of us, and have been waiting for the rest of us to catch up.

And teaching a younger generation of Christians to care for creation is one of the things that will help to turn the corner on the environmental crisis for all humanity. The crisis is theoretically solvable. A number of writers are cautiously optimistic that if the right decisions are made within the next few years, the human race can survive. Climate-changing greenhouse gases can be curtailed. The growth of the human population is beginning to slow and it is now possible to see beyond its peak and to plan for a truly sustainable future. But a lot of work needs to be done, and that work will be done or not done by our children and grandchildren. Will the children and grandchildren of today's Bible-believing Christians be part of this? I hope so. I hope they will be leading the way, and that they will do so because of what they learned in Sunday school rather than in spite of it. What do we need to do?

### Leaders make the difference

When we talk about Christian Ed and Youth Programs, our minds first to go materials. Is there a curriculum we can use? There is a place for teaching material, but more important than anything else will be having leaders and teachers of young children who understand what God's world is about, who care about it and can convey that passion to the young people they are teaching.

Your church might have such leaders already. Maybe you are one and that's why you're reading this book. If not, the best way to start is to go back one chapter. A church that is bringing creation care into worship, preaching and teaching on the adult level will soon have Sunday school teachers and youth leaders who can do the same thing for young people.

We can't teach what we don't understand. We will never convey a love for something we don't love ourselves.

## Creation care in children's programs

One of the most successful programs at Au Sable Institute in Michigan is an outreach to public school children. This innovative program is almost 30 years old, and has seen several generations of children from all of the surrounding communities come every year from kindergarten through eighth grade for day-long field trips. The program integrates age-specific topics with the State of Michigan's standard science curriculum recommendations for each grade level. Because the children are coming from public schools, the program's teachers do not put Christian content into the lessons—but they don't need to. God's creation has a way of opening minds as nothing else can.

Program Director Patricia Fagg explains:

> *Within the context of our environmental education program we strive to inspire as well as instruct-to train the heart as well as the head. This type of training is best done through direct experiences in the outdoors. Through the Au Sable program we try to reach each student's imagination, to stir the student's heart and mind, to awaken enthusiasm, to pique curiosity, and to evoke feeling and action. We try to set the stage so our students will want to know more, will want to discover on their own, and will seek out deeper meanings and understandings.*
> [www.ausable.org/cp.gl.eep.goals.cfm]

Patricia is not only an educator—she is a scientist in her own right. Few Sunday school teachers, youth leaders or college professors could match her. But almost anyone can do what she is doing. All you need is children, and grass and trees, and maybe a pond or stream. It isn't necessary to have a full science curriculum, for the goal is creation-appreciation, not detailed scientific analysis. There is so much to know and learn in creation that it doesn't matter if the teacher doesn't know a lot more than the students; what is wanted is a love and an excitement about God's world. Such things are contagious. And the students will respond and they will remember. Long after Bible verses have faded, the wonders of creatures in pond water will still be an exciting memory.

My suggestions have a certain parallel to those for the worship program in the last chapter:

- *Take the children into creation.* Get out of doors. God made the sky—he didn't make the ceiling. Go to a park near the church. Explore the stream that borders the property—you can talk about the ducks or you can talk about the old tires or both. Get an idea of the wonders in the world—find things that are amazing and cool—and help them to feel the sadness when that world is damaged, polluted, destroyed. Go easy on the bible verses—creation has a pretty clear voice when we let her speak on her own. (It will be the easiest class you ever taught.)

- *Bring creation in when you can't go out.* Bring in some unusual pets to show how amazing they are and how amazing God is. Someone at church has a job that relates to creation. Pull them in to talk to your kids. Set up an ant farm. Find ways to let creation speak on her own, and your kids will listen.

- *Instill a sense of environmental responsibility.* Little things matter and children notice little things like lights left on. Children who see energy waste as a sin when they are six will turn off the lights when they are eighteen. They will take the message home more effectively than any bill insert from the power company.

- *Encourage further study of creation at the library or at school.* An hour a week might whet a young person's appetite, but will hardly satisfy a hungry mind. Convey over and over the idea that God's word and God's world are two volumes of the same book.

These are little things; the goal isn't very sophisticated—a simple appreciation of God's world is sufficient. But it's important. Kids who love God's world will grow up to care about it. Those who don't, won't.

### Creation care for youth

The first church which I served as Pastor was small enough that I had the privilege of multitasking as only the pastor of such a church would understand. Running the mimeograph machine (this was a long time ago), serving communion, preaching the sermon and leading the youth group. I got to do it all. Especially leading the youth group: Spending time with those junior high and high school kids saved my sanity more than once in the five years I spent at that church.

We spent a lot of time outdoors. Annual canoe trips on the Ipswich River north of Boston. Mountain climbing in the New Hampshire White Mountains. Sometimes, in the fall or spring, just chucking the day's lesson in favor of a walk through the golf course that bordered our church property. Those kids—almost middle aged adults now—still talk about the time Lisa (a 15 year old) and I upset our canoe, and I was accused of trying to get her baptized.

I used to think I was cheating. I had no grand agenda for bringing creation care into the youth program. No one had ever used the term at that time. Sometimes it was just easier to go for a walk with 15 kids than to try to keep them occupied in a stuffy classroom. But I'm thinking about those experiences, years later. I can remember the mountain climbs. I can remember the canoe trips. I can even recall some of the walks on the golf course. I recall very little of what went on in the classroom. And I would not be surprised if the kids who were part of the group at that time agreed with me.

Most youth programs spend plenty of time outdoors. It's a question of survival for the leaders—the amount of energy a group of middle school or high school students can generate requires lots of space and plenty of air. So we are out in God's classroom much of the time already. While it isn't a problem to use God's world as a backdrop for a game of capture-the-flag, there are many other opportunities that we don't want to miss:

- *Let creation speak.* A thunderstorm in the middle of a hike, an unexpected encounter with deer around the corner, even the sight of a polluted stream or an abandoned car in the middle of "wild nature"—all of these are opportunities to discuss God, creation, and humanity. Use the Bible, but appropriately. The most powerful experiences of God's presence in creation relate better to Psalm 19 than to John 3:16 or Romans 1:17. Letting creation groan is useful, too. A visit to your regional sanitary landfill would be a lesson in waste and consumption that the students (and you) will never forget.

- *Let the students speak.* A hike, a canoe trip, a quiet evening at the end of mission-trip day watching the sunset. When creation speaks, we need to have an opportunity to share with each other what we are hearing. Provide sharing times out under the stars, or if camping, as the sun comes up. These are precious times, especially if you are ministering in an urban or highly structured suburban setting.

- *Teach creation care values.* "Take nothing but pictures. Leave nothing but footprints."' This is a common sign at the start of a nature trail, but your kids will walk right past it. Use the opportunity to teach. "We take nothing and we leave nothing because *we know the Creator*, and we're taking care of it for him."

Youth programs represent an opportunity to move beyond creation-appreciation into the actual care for and healing of creation. If your youth program is at all typical, you are already doing both local service projects and cross-cultural mission trips on a regular basis. These can easily be integrated with a creation care ministry philosophy:

- *Use service project time for environmental projects.* "Adopt a highway" is a common project around the country now, but I would rather see you "adopt a stream" or "adopt a trail" even if no one gives you a fancy sign as a reward for your work. God didn't make the highway, and no matter how much litter you pick up, fish or birds or voles will never be welcome there. Google for "environmental volunteer opportunities" in your region, or call the Department of Natural Resources or the Parks Department. Try to go back to the same stream or trail annually or more often and you will begin to see your investment in effort pay off.

- *Include creation-teaching moments on mission trips.* If you're going to another country, do some research on the state of that country's environment. Make sure your team members see the damage that is being done to God's creation in that country, and how that damage is hurting the people you've come to serve. If you're traveling in the US, be sure that your side trips include opportunities to experience the wonders of God's great open spaces.

- I'm sure you already do this, but if not, *ban iPods and every other device that might block creation's song* on trips. Your kids have been immersed in their consumer youth culture for years, and it won't be easy to pull them out of its grasp. But if you can't do it, no one can.

- *Do some career counseling.* Kids are starting to wonder what God wants them to do or to be. Look for the Cal DeWitt or the Frances Collins in your group. Rather than scaring them away from science because of fears that they might encounter philosophies or teachings they've never heard before, encourage them! We desperately need scientists who are Christians, and these might be the very children you are taking on walks right now. You never know where they might end up with your help. You could be invited to a Nobel Prize award ceremony.

### Creation care at Camp

Camping doesn't usually occur in local church settings. But camping ministries serve young people (and often adult groups as well) from local churches. Christian camping and retreat centers represent a substantial ministry effort that reaches thousands of young people and many not so young every year. You could not find a better setting in which to teach about God's creation. The greatest barrier to teaching creation care in any other ministry setting is absent here: Creation is all around us; we are already in the classroom. Everything that we have to make an effort to achieve back in the Sunday school classroom is right in front of us.

How effectively are we using God's creation as a classroom setting? A friend of mine, speaking on this topic at a convention for Christian camping ministries, posed a question for these ministry leaders to consider: Could you run your program in a gym? If you can, you are not using the resources and advantages God has given you.

How might a camp setting promote creation care?

- *Bring the background to center stage.* Instead of using creation like a set of drapes, make it the main attraction. Set up a program that lets the kids explore the world around them. A row of inexpensive microscopes and some jars of pond water. Binoculars and bird books. Magnifying glasses for examining the bugs under the rocks just outside the cabin door. A program built on creation instead of using it as a backdrop would be easy to teach and would generate its own excitement. Why spend time (and money) making craft projects that will be broken or lost before the summer is over when we could start at young person on a life time of bird watching or plant identification and teach a lot more about God in the process.

- *Bring a scientist on staff.* You will want someone with experience teaching kids in the outdoors who probably has a biology or environmental science degree. A number of Christian colleges produce such graduates every year—and some of them would just love to spend their summers showing kids the wonders of bugs. Talented undergraduates could serve as nature counselors as well. These students obviously won't stay around, but a partnership with Au Sable Institute or one of the Christian colleges could provide a steady stream of young and enthusiastic staff members to whet the appetites of your campers.

- *Build your bible teaching programs around creation care.* As with the church program, worship and study of the written word helps us understand and interpret the created world.

- *Find out who is doing interesting things in creation near your camp, and incorporate them into your program.* Take the campers to visit the fish hatchery, or visit an organic farm (or even a not so organic one). Make a field trip out of cleaning up trails in the local state park. Teach your campers that caring for God's creation both important and fun.

- *Incorporate principles of creation care in facility management and foodservice.* Compost your waste. When you have to build or landscape, use the best techniques available. Be energy conscious. Use camper-labor to rid your land of dangerous exotic weeds. Eat "low on the food chain"—more vegetables, less meat. And let your campers and their parents know that caring for God's creation is one of your organization's core values. You might be surprised at the response you get, and you might find that a well-advertised "green Christian camping" program will even attract parents and children who are not so interested in church, but who do care about God's world.

As we have already said, in business "green business" is good business. In the competitive world of camping, "green camping" is good ministry strategy.


## Creation care on campus

The last thirty years have dramatically changed the environmental studies landscape at Christian colleges. At the beginning of that time period, no Christian colleges offered majors in environmental science. Few offered courses in the subject and there were no fulltime faculty in this field. Today, fifty-seven colleges are affiliated with Au Sable Institute of Environmental Studies. Many of these offer an Environmental Science or Environmental Studies major and have dedicated faculty. Several of the larger schools have their own environmental field stations. And environmental activities at these colleges go beyond the classroom. A number of schools—Gordon and Messiah are examples—have active, campus wide recycling programs. The science divisions of our Christian colleges are leading the rest of the evangelical community in caring for God's creation.

However, with the possible exception of the recycling programs, creation care often does not extend beyond the doors of the science buildings. Many of the environmental science faculty members are struggling, often alone, to bring the message of creation care to the mainstream of college life. This is not surprising, since campuses will reflect the attitudes and priorities of the churches from which the students come, but it has to change. Colleges and seminaries have often led the rest of the evangelical community, and can do so again.

The scientists have done their part. We know from them what the problems are, and we have a good handle on some of the solutions that can be deployed. But the environment will not be fixed by scientists. It will be fixed by business leaders, politicians and pastors. Especially by pastors. Few people will exert more influence for good or for ill than the leaders of tomorrow's congregations. And we know exactly where these future leaders are: They are in class right now, in Bible College and Seminary. They are studying Greek and Hebrew and Homiletics and Systematic Theology and Counseling and Youth Ministry and ... almost everything but Environmental Theology or Creation Care.

We need Christian colleges and seminaries to review their programs in light of the need to mobilize the church for this crisis. This could begin with regular chapel programs and hosted conferences, but should ultimately require every future pastor to have a course in creation care theology.

The students in class today will influence the entire church community—and our nation and world—toward or away from a healthy attitude toward God's creation and an adequate response to the environmental crisis.

# nine

## GODLY AND GREEN

I've already told you a couple of stories about my church-going experiences. I like my church. The pastor and I get along. Teaching is good. The staff seems to be hard working and dedicated. There are reasons that this church is exploding—it is a fun and vibrant place to worship and connect with other Christians. Blackhawk Church has what many would consider a good problem, but it is still a problem, as the pastor will be happy to tell you. Too many people are showing up for worship. The facility was designed for about 500 people—and more than 2500 now attend 9 services from 8 AM to 7 PM every Sunday. Parking is a challenge and relationships with the neighbors are understandably frayed. Would you want to live across a narrow street from a church packing in 2500 people? In spite of the best efforts of an army of volunteers and repeated announcements in church, God's people still block driveways, create muddy ruts on the edge of the road, and generally make life difficult for those who have to live here.

What's a church to do? Moving appears to be the only answer—you can't discourage people from attending. The mission of the church in general and this church in particular, calls for an open door and an invitation that is as physical as it is spiritual: "Whoever will may come." So our church is moving. Several months ago we broke ground on a piece of property well outside the current development boundaries of our already sprawling city. What was pasture and cornfield last year is now a muddy building site, and by this time next year will be the new home of Blackhawk Church.

Please understand: I am not questioning the decision to build, or where the new building is going to be, or even how the building is going up. A variety of other options were considered before making the final decision. A site was selected in careful coordination with city authorities, who already had plans for the development of the new area. City and church are working closely to implement a number of the principles of new urbanism including sharing parking facilities with neighboring businesses. And the building itself will incorporate a variety of principles advocated by the LEED (Leadership in Energy and Environmental Design—see below) building system, though cost is preventing full LEED certification. I don't know that I would have done anything differently.

But still. Another farm is being ploughed under for suburban buildings and a parking garage. Most people will have to drive further than they do now to go to church, unless they move into some of the several thousand new houses going up in the same neighborhood in the next couple of years. All this shows that it isn't any easier to put creation care principles into practice at church than it is at home or at work. Whether your church is growing into a new building as we are, or is rattling around in a 150 year old mausoleum, it isn't easy to be green.

*Mobilizing the church means applying creation care principles in the siting, design and operation of our church buildings and grounds.* It is manifestly true that "the building is not the church—the people are", but the facilities that a church is housed in are important. Like your own physical body, they are the visible, public face of the church. Church facilities that squander energy or are surrounded by acres of parking and green lawns soaked in chemical poisons are an embarrassment to the glory and reputation of the God they represent. It is not easy to bring our church facilities into line with what we are learning about creation care principles. But some things can be done. Here's how.

## Church planting is green

A common term for starting new churches is beautifully ecological: "church planting". You probably haven't thought of church planting as a way to reduce your churchs impact on creation—but why not? The biggest consumption of energy in a large church is probably the fuel used by the cars in the parking lot, and one of the biggest challenges to church attendance in the next twenty five years will unquestionably be the cost of driving. Large churches today tend to follow a shopping mall model—large facilities that draw from a very large area. In a future marked by very high transportation costs, the McDonald's model may turn out to be a necessity—smaller, neighborhood based facilities to which people can walk or drive a short distance.

It's just a suggestion. "Planting" is always greener than "building".

## Designing for worship

As I approached the church where I was scheduled to speak, I had seldom seen one in a prettier setting. Built on a hill overlooking a highway, it was nestled against a patch of trees. Standing outside the front door, I could see beautiful Wisconsin countryside for miles on three sides. But when I entered the sanctuary, all of that disappeared. Moderate in size, seating maybe 200 people, it was of fairly recent construction, and had narrow windows on one side. And all of the windows were covered with blinds. You got just a hint that the sun was shining, but no more. It didn't matter what the weather was like. It could have been a cloudy, rainy day—it could have been snowing in August. We would not have known. God's world was completely shut out from our worship.

I know why we do this. Projected images appear brighter when the windows are shaded. There are fewer distractions when we can't see the world outside, so we can focus better on the worship service. Well, maybe. Imagine your feelings if you walked into a church and the greeter at the door took a look at the Bible in your hands and said to you, "Welcome to our church! In order to avoid distractions during the message, we'd like to ask you to leave your Bible here. You can collect it again when you leave" Absurd. Illogical. How could having a Bible distract me from worship? But that is what we do when we design worship spaces that shut out even a hint of God's creation. We are cutting ourselves off from that 'other book'.

Let's begin by bringing creation back into the worship area. Let's design with natural light and with windows so we can see God's sky and experience his weather and respond to the changes of the seasons as the year progresses. Such a setting can enhance the worship experience in some unexpected ways. Some years ago I was preaching in a community church that was meeting at the time in a Catholic monastery. The chapel that we were using had windows set high in the south wall in such a way that the sun could shine into the middle of the hall. It happened to be a cloudy day, but just as I reached a particularly emphatic point in the message, the clouds broke and the sun burst through as if God himself was saying, "Listen up! This is important!" The congregation seemed to get the message. Worship spaces designed for total human control of lighting and sound inevitably remove God's Spirit from the equation. We are the poorer for it.

Some suggestions for the design or renovation of worship spaces in a way that will allow God's creation to have a voice in our worship:

- *If you are building, select a site—or the worship space on your site—to allow views of creation instead of man-made structures.* You might not have a choice, but if you do and can, the effort will be rewarded.

- *Place windows to allow a view of the outside world, and to reduce or eliminate the need for daytime lighting.* Windows don't have to eliminate the possibility of projecting song lyrics new projectors are bright enough to handle normal room light if placed properly.

- *If you are in an urban setting, with only manmade structures, you can still put some creative landscaping around your windows, or where the windows will be when you're done.* How about a green belt between the windows and the streets. You might find that soon God will send some of his birds to liven up the space.

- *Incorporate elements of creation in the interior design.* Plastic plants are to real ones what paper plates are to fine china. You can tell the difference! Enough said.

Similar principles can be applied to other areas of the church, of course, such as fellowship areas, lobbies, classrooms. Make it so that everyone who enters the building sees the connection between God and his world. And don't forget to make that connection clear in the worship and teaching that goes on here.

### *Lead with* LEED

If you are building—if you must build—become familiar with the LEED program. *Leadership in Energy and Environmental Design,* sponsored by the US Green Building Council[1] is a comprehensive, point-based certification program to encourage new construction (and renovation projects) that is appropriate and based on the best current 'green' thinking. LEED certification is expensive—levels range from "Certified" through

---

[1] www.usgbc.org

"Platinum", and points are awarded for every aspect of construction, from site preparation and disposal of building materials to energy conservation and sourcing of the materials used in construction. A LEED certified church building would be a powerful statement to a community that "this congregation cares". Even if you can't afford full certification, get your building committee and contractor to study the principles and to see how many you can implement.

As of this writing, LEED is mostly oriented toward commercial office structures—certainly applicable if you are building a large, suburban church building. They are in the process of developing a LEED for Schools program that will probably be quite applicable to churches when available.

*Operating as stewards*

Rev. Charles Morris and the St. Elizabeth Catholic Church in Wyandotte, Michigan, found their way into the pages of the *New York Times* recently. If you visit this suburb of Detroit you can find the church by looking for the windmill—and the solar panels on the roof, the front porch and the garage. According to the *Times*, Father Morris has reduced his congregation's annual energy bills by more than $ 20,000 per year. Says Father Morris, "We're all part of God's creation. If someone like me doesn't speak about its care, who will? The changes we've made here, that's a form of preaching."

Energy use is a moral issue. We are entering a period of global energy scarcity as indicated by the rapid increase in the world cost of oil. Occasional 'declines' in the price of oil, when they occur, simply emphasize the point. Not many years ago, a rise to current levels would have been shocking. Energy prices are driven by one thing: demand. As painful as the cost of energy may be for you and me, it is much more painful for our brothers and sisters in other, poorer parts of the world. Every unit of energy we use we buy in competition with other users who have much less than we do. Our demand drives the price of their energy up, as well as our own. Minimizing the use of energy in our church buildings as well as our vehicles and our homes is a moral issue because every unit of energy we use is taken from someone else who needs it, as much or more than we do, and every unit we save is available for others to use.

Use of energy from fossil fuels is also the major driving force behind global climate change. Every puff of greenhouse gas that your church pumps into the atmosphere adds to the problems being caused by climate change, increasing future damage on God's creation for your children, your grandchildren, and your Christian brothers and sisters around the world. It is simple to help. All we have to do is reduce the amount of energy we're using. And at the same time, we can check with our local utility to see if it is possible to purchase green power' from sources like wind. Many utilities now offer this as an option.

There are few better places to demonstrate stewardship and "loving our neighbors" than in how we operate our church facilities. Most church buildings are big. They use a lot of energy—heat in the winter, electricity for air conditioning in the summer, lighting all year long. We purchase commercial chemicals for cleaning, and flush the residue into the water system. The opportunities are clear—and the benefits are substantial. It costs nothing to be good stewards—it's almost always an effort that results in substantial monetary savings.

- *Heat and air conditioning:* Get a professional review, and make the investment needed to update your systems. Computerized building controls, new high efficiency HVAC units will almost always pay for themselves quickly.

- *Building insulation.* Keep the energy you've already expended inside. Enough said.

- *Lighting:* I hope you've already switched from incandescent to new long-life fluorescent bulbs. Great progress has been made in lighting technology in the last few years.

- *Office machines:* Turn them off at night. Be sure all of your computers are set to shut off the monitor after 15 minutes and hard disks after 30. And if you turn off the power strip itself, you will eliminate the "phantom load" from standby power. 10 % reduction in energy use is almost guaranteed. (Your machines will last longer, too.)

- *Use "green" cleaning supplies.* It might take a bit of research on the web, but the effort will be worth it.

- *Switch to reusable cups, mugs, dishes, etc.* One easy way to do this—get people to bring their own. It would be an unusual commuter who doesn't have a travel mug that he or she uses all week long. Why not on Sunday as well? Not very many years ago, standard church dinner procedure was "bring a dish to share—and bring your own dishes to eat from". This will eliminate work in the church kitchen, the cost of disposable dishes and a lot of waste. Why send God's money out the back door in trash bags to mess up his world?

### Glorifying God on the grounds

The retention pond at Door Creek church was just plain ugly. It was required by the city to help control storm water runoff, but it looked like a huge storm drain, sitting at front of the property as you drove up. It had been neglected while the new building was being built, and had even received some unwanted building materials from the church construction and from other houses being built in the neighborhood. The pond added nothing to the attractiveness of the church grounds, and to some like my friend Paul, it was an embarrassment.

Paul knew that it didn't have to be like that. He had done restoration work on his own rural property, and he was a member of a local prairie restoration group. He discovered that there was a temporary gap in church oversight—no one was in charge of that part of the grounds—and he gathered a group of people and got to work. There were church members who were landscapers and someone with connections to the city Parks Department who was able to secure prairie plants. The area was cleaned and planted with native plants. Today that ignored and ugly piece of land is charming and beautiful and full of God's flowers, birds and wildlife. It recently became something more for the congregation: A memorial garden where church members remember their family members with the donation of a tree or shrub, marked by a boulder carved with a favorite Bible verse.

The day I visited Door Creek to have a look at this effort at creation celebration, five or six people were in the process of burning the prairie. Prairies like fire—plants that shouldn't be there are removed, the ash fertilizes the soil, and some prairie plants can't even germinate until they feel the heat of a prairie fire. It is another example of the complex system God has established for different parts of his creation. Six years after beginning the work of transforming an ugly storm ditch and construction dump, Door Creek's memorial prairie is now the most beautiful part of the church grounds, and home to dozens of kinds of birds and fish—and probably many small mammals as well.

The property that surrounds our church buildings should be a place where God's creation is celebrated. But if your church is typical, your church property is comprised of parking lots, lawns and landscaping shrubbery and not much else. Nothing grows on a parking lot, and your green areas are probably soaked in chemical poisons to keep the grass green and to kill everything that wants to compete with it  plant, animal or insect. I wonder if this is really the best return on investment for the Owner of the property? None of us intend to do harm to God's creatures when we set out to have attractive landscaping that fits in with the suburban culture that surrounds many of our church buildings. We want to enhance the reputation and ministry of the church. But when we manage church property 'just like everyone else' we become part of the problem. Our lawn chemicals are silently destroying God's worship choir while we're inside singing,

> *All things bright and beautiful,*
> *All creatures great and small,*
> *All things wise and wonderful,*
> *The Lord God made them all . . .*

But something even more significant is going on. A church surrounded by nothing but parking lots and suburban grass is squandering an opportunity to bring glory to God when it could be creating a place for God's creatures to live, a place that could then be used by people who are looking for God in his world. It doesn't take a lot of space to create a patch of trees and shrubbery that can be homes for dozens of kinds of birds, squirrels, rabbits and many other wonderful creeping and crawling things. Your church property might already have some pockets of left-over creation—corners of the property you haven't "developed" yet. Or you could bring in trees and plants as Door Creek church did. Put in walkways and benches. Make an 'outdoor classroom' that Christian Education or youth groups can use regularly. Learn to chase out the exotic weeds and bring in the kinds of native plants that God designed for your neighborhood. And invite your neighbors to come and enjoy God's good earth with you. You might even find that some of them enjoy your outdoor worship space so much they decide to see what's goes on inside.

Some quick suggestions to help glorify God on your church grounds:

- *Develop a multiple-use management plan for your church grounds.*
  In most of our churches, the grounds are a giant welcome mat leading to the front door and not much more. This is a waste. Parking is essential, but it may be one of the least important contributions your property can make to advance the mission of the church. Go back to the sections on worship and education, and look at your church property again as a potential extension of those ministries.

- *Minimize artificial landscaping like lawns, and maximize natural areas that are just as attractive, less expensive to maintain, and give God's creatures places to live.* In Wisconsin, prairies are popular because they are native. In your region, it might be a New England wooded area or a desert cactus garden. Lawn and garden experts in your community would love to help  some of them might even be in your congregation. If we put back what God used to have here, God's creatures will come back on their own. Just give them a chance!

- *Where you have to have lawns and parking, use materials and methods that will do the least possible damage to the soil and creatures.* Lawns can be managed without chemicals—for ideas and suggestions, check www.safelawns.org.  Recent improvements in parking lot technology include porous pavement—materials that allow rainwater to soak through into the ground, and grasscrete—cement tiles with spaces for grass and plants to grow through, but with the strength to support vehicles.

### Bringing creation to an inner-city church setting

I was encouraging a group of pastors with some of the suggestions I have mentioned here.  One man raised his hand: "When I look out of my church's windows, all I see is a parking lot and a gas station. Is that what you have in mind?" His urban church was meeting in a store front. He had plenty of windows already—but the view outside was nothing that would bring glory to God or enhance worship.

Urban church settings represent unique challenges—but no one needs a touch of God's creation more than those who are living, working and worshiping in the city.  But if you live in the city, you will already have noticed that creation dies hard. Every sidewalk, empty lot and polluted stream shows plants struggling to live and to sing praises to the creator. As long as we are in the city as well, let's try to help them grow by giving them space.

Every urban situation is going to be different, but here are some thoughts to get you started:

- *Try to make creation visible from your worship space.* Windows to let in light can be shielded from the gas station or graffiti with a screen of plants outside, inside or both.

- *Adopt an empty lot nearby for a community garden.* (See the chapter on community outreach.)

- *Adopt a park or stream and get your youth group or Sunday school classes to tend it.* Not "clean it up." That's a one-time effort and usually not very satisfactory. Tending implies going back over and over again, and seeing the accumulated results of your efforts. Much more satisfying.

- If you can afford it financially, try to get people out of the city to a state or county park for worship, not just for fun. *You know what I mean—have fun, but make the experience meaningful as well.*

The building and grounds are not the church—but they are the visible body that the community sees, and they are small parts of the great worship space called creation. What we do with them matters and what we do with them can make all the difference in how we and those around us learn to see God in his world, and how to care for that world.

# ten

# LOVING OUR COMMUNITIES

When Pastor Tri Robinson followed his convictions and finally preached a sermon on environmental stewardship at his
church in Boise Idaho, he admits that he was terrified. But he
also knew that one sermon by itself would mean nothing. If
this truth—that God's people have to care for God's earth—
was important, it had to become a visible reality in people's
lives. And it did. Huge recycling bins line one side of the Boise
Vineyard parking lot. "Tithe your trash" brings in hundreds
of pounds of recyclables every week. Recycling containers are
prominent throughout the church campus complex. Teams of
church volunteers regularly arrive at nearby National Park Service trailheads to do trail maintenance, plant trees and assist
the park service in caring for some of the wilderness areas with
which Idaho is blessed. The church's outreach to victims of
Katrina was funded in part by a church effort to collect and recycle cell phones throughout the city, a program that resulted
in a number of community members arriving at the church on
Sunday morning to find out what this 'green' congregation was
all about.

## Healing starts at home

*Mobilizing the church means becoming active in practical creation care projects in our local communities.* Integrating creation care in worship and education programs is an essential first step, and incorporating creation care principles in how church facilities run is only common sense. Both of these are only a start. We have a world that has been damaged, and we have to be involved in the healing process. The way you and I live actively contributes to the abuse of God's creation. If we are serious about this problem, we have to move from worship services to service projects that will begin to reverse the damage and make a difference.

Madison, Wisconsin, my own little corner of God's creation, is far from an environmental basket case. The State of Wisconsin has a strong interest in protecting forests and wildlife, and has been the recipient of a number of 'quality of life' awards. But even here, trouble is not far beneath the surface:

- *After thinking for years that we had some of the best water in the country, we've recently learned that we don't. There are contamination problems in a number of our wells.*

- *All of our lakes suffer from the over fertilization of suburban lawns and are being overrun by a variety of plant and animal exotic species, including Eurasian water milfoil and the infamous zebra mussel.*

- *Our woodland is overrun by a noxious weed called garlic mustard, and mature trees throughout the state are in danger from a tiny insect called the 'ash borer'. Acid rain threatens, though most of 'our' acid rain falls in Michigan.*

- *Farmland throughout the area is being swallowed by housing developments and 'big box' retail development.*

- *We are running one of the dirtiest power plants in Wisconsin just 3 blocks from the Wisconsin Capitol building.*

None of this compares with the body blows creation is taking in Kenya, Haiti and many other countries—but these are still wounds to my little corner of God's world. Some of them I can do something about. A list for your community will be different. It might be longer but I would be very surprised if it was any shorter. If your corner of God's creation is hurting, it's your responsibility, because it's where God has placed you right now.

### *Loving creation is loving your neighbor*

There is another reason why we should be looking for creation care service opportunities in our communities. This is something that many members of our communities care deeply about. They are matters that affect 'the common good' of all of us. When a church professes to love its neighbors, but doesn't care about the water or trees, those neighbors can hardly be criticized for questioning the sincerity of that love. Ignoring creation care issues results in a deep disconnect that undermines efforts to reach our communities.

A church that is active in caring for all of creation will be appreciated and will find genuine and increasing respect for its message of eternal redemption. Activities that heal creation— and even better, that lead in communitywide creation care efforts will bring people into the church that otherwise would never enter the door of a church. Many of those who are involved in environmental stewardship projects at the local level are young, idealistic, and passionate. They need meaning in their lives, something to do and something love, and they have found it in a passion for God's creation—even though they don't know that that is what it is. They are without deep philosophical (read theological if you like) reasons for what they are doing, but they know things are going badly in nature and they want to fix them. They are easily discouraged because the problems are too big; the powers that be are distant and daunting.

People like this have half a foot inside the door to God's kingdom already. Imagine a gospel message that connects their instinctive care for God's creation with his eternal work of redemption through Jesus Christ.

Your community creation care program will be different from mine, because the problems and the people are different. Anything a church does in its own community needs to be done in response to the needs in that community at that time. Boise Vineyard established a recycling program as one of its first efforts because there are few if any communitywide recycling programs in the Boise area. My own community has a convenient and efficient curbside recycling program put in place by the city. A Madison church would not want to start its own recycling program, but could find many other ways to be active.

Generally, creation care activities should fall into three categories. Note that there is a direct connection between this list and some of the material we discussed previously in the chapters on worship and creation care for the next generation:

- *Creation Appreciation.* We need to spend time learning about what we want to save. Whether the creatures in the woodland that borders a city park, or the birds that visit on their annual pilgrimages north or south, few of us know or appreciate much about God's world. What we don't know we can't appreciate. What we don't appreciate we won't care about. What we don't care about we won't try to fix or to save. Many of the activities we have discussed previously—outdoor worship services, outdoor Sunday school classes and youth group meetings, nature walks—will accomplish this goal. But similar events could be planned for and with the rest of your community. Earth Day comes every April, and is often close to Easter. This is a natural time to connect with the rest of the community.

- *Creation Healing.* There are many things that can be done in every community to bring healing and restoration on a practical level. Almost all of them require little skill but a lot of people. And generally our churches are good at jobs that take people power—because that's part of what we are about. Pulling noxious weeds like garlic mustard, cleaning trash from stream beds, planting trees or prairie plants, clearing and maintaining hiking trails are all examples of ways that the man-, woman- and child-power of your congregation can make a meaningful contribution to the health of your corner of God's creation.

- *Lifestyle transformation programs.* Many of the larger problems in creation—energy use, climate change, and the negative effects of a consumer lifestyle—can only be solved by changing the way we live. Changing is easier when you do it together. Churches can encourage appropriate lifestyle changes in a variety of ways: Encourage carpooling and the use of public transport. Sponsor bike to church' days. Collect specialized items for recycling that public programs won't handle like batteries, cell phones and printer ink cartridges. Cell phones and cartridges can be sold for a nice source of income for one of the church mission projects or youth programs.

I was once part of a church that tried to serve the community every year at Christmas time by providing free gift-wrapping in one of the shopping malls. This was a sincere attempt to express unconditional love by doing something for people, but I could never get very excited about it. What were we really doing but giving people who already had more than enough something that any of them could have done on their own—as well as aiding and abetting them in their consumer-driven lifestyles. We may have been serving—but we weren't helping. How much better to find a project that serves by healing creation, and so genuinely helps the whole community's quality of life to improve and that inevitably draws people to the Creator.

# eleven

## A HEALING MISSION

$M$issions is changing. How true this is came home to me recently when I read a note from a missionary language school in Pakistan—the same school at which my own parents learned the languages of Sindhi and Urdu fifty years ago, and which at that time was almost entirely populated with North American missionaries. Today, I learned, the new, young missionaries studying in that school are almost all from Korea and China. Yesterday's "mission fields" have become today's "mission senders". Missions in the 20th Century truly represents one of the greatest success stories in church history. If the goal was to plant churches and make disciples around the world, we have done that—to the point where those planted churches are sending out missionaries of their own.

Unfortunately, in the words of missionary statesman Ralph Winter, we may be looking at a case where "the operation was successful but the patient died", for many countries where the missionary effort has been most active and spiritually most effective are now in terrible shape economically, politically and environmentally. In Guatemala, where Winter spent the early years of his career, the children and grandchildren of his early converts are among thousands who risk their lives to enter and work illegally in the United States because conditions in their home regions have deteriorated to the point where they can no longer support their families on ancestral land and there are no jobs. Almost all cash income in the region is in the form of remittances from family members working in the US. Families are separated, in many cases with all working age male members away from home.

Consider Haiti. Close to the North American mainland, Haiti has been a favorite destination for short term missions trips, youth group mission teams and extensive development and church planting efforts. Hundreds of organizations and thousands of individual Christians have taken part in efforts to reach and serve Haiti. Few countries in the world have enjoyed greater attention from the North American Christian missions effort than this small island nation. In spite of all that effort, Haiti is one of the most crisis-ridden countries on earth. Wracked with violence, afflicted by a series of governments, each exceeding its predecessor in incompetence and corruption, Haiti also represents one of the worst cases of environmental collapse in the modern world. Ninety-seven percent of forest has been cut down. Agricultural land is washing into the sea. Tropical storms that kill dozens on neighboring islands kill hundreds and thousands on Haiti. Without forests and soil, there is nothing to absorb the rainfall, and flash floods and mudslides are the rule. The security situation is at the point that many missionary efforts have been sharply curtailed and in some instances have ceased because of the difficulty of protecting staff. Jared Diamond sums Haiti up in one sentence: "The question that all visitors to Haiti ask themselves is whether there is any hope for the country, and the usual answer is 'no'." [Diamond 2005, 330]

In Kenya, where *Care of Creation* is at work, is not as desperate as Haiti—at least not yet. But many of the same elements are present. Rapid population growth, serious deforestation, decline of agricultural productivity due to erosion and loss of fertility on the land that is left means that today a greater percentage of the population of Kenya lives below the poverty line than when missionaries first arrived. The missionary effort has been 'successful'—the churches are full of enthusiastic worshipers—but the land is hurting, the people are suffering, and it doesn't take much imagination to see a Kenya ten or fifteen years from now that looks much like Haiti does today.

I know these are complicated situations. There are many different factors at work, and the failure or absence of economic, government and environmental policies is evident. I can't help but wonder, though, if a more complete gospel at the start—one that taught the kind of respect for God's creation that we have been discussing throughout this book—might have helped a bit. However we arrived at this point, we are here now, and we have to face the fact that many of the countries most affected by environmental crises right now are countries where we have spent millions of dollars in evangelism and church planting. These are our Christian brothers and sisters. What will we do about it?

*Mobilizing the church means responding to the environmental crisis in other countries as an act of love toward brothers and sisters in Jesus.* This response needs to occur on two levels. In our churches in North America and other 'sending' countries, we need to become aware of the reality of the international environmental crisis and include environmental ministries–like Care of Creation, Floresta and A Rocha—in our mission budgets. Christian environmental projects need to be funded and expanded. Equally important, mission agencies and Christian organizations of all kinds need to adapt their outreach and development strategies to include creation care—projects, for immediate assistance and teaching to establish a biblical foundation for ongoing creation care in the community. Remember my ship story: If the ship goes down, all the other programs go down with it.

What if we were to establish a new model of missions that would set out to both reach people and to bring Jesus' redemption and reconciliation to the land, air, water and all of God's creatures? What would that look like? Here are some ideas that are designed for those, like Care of Creation, who are working in on these problems. I hope, though that some of you 'back home' will review these as well, and consider how you can encourage the missionaries and the organizations you already support to direct their efforts in this direction.

### Sound theology

First, we have to be sure that creation care mission efforts, like any other kind, are *theologically sound*. That is, we have to ensure that our missionary theology includes everything we've been talking about in this book: Believing and teaching that God made the world for himself, that how we treat creation matters deeply to God and is often a matter of life and death for those living in the countries we are seeking to reach. Bad or incomplete theology leads to bad results, but good theology will result in comprehensive, holistic approaches to mission outreach efforts.

Sound theology will keep bringing us back to the root causes of the problems we face. It is easy to get so focused on the practical challenges of tree planting, for example, that we lose sight of the sin problems we are trying to deal with. Environmental problems are sin problems but they don't present themselves that way. Erosion on a farm may be the result of sinful neglect, but it looks like muddy fields washing away. Deforested hillsides need to be addressed with boots and gloves. Diseases caused by environmental pollution need clinics and new government policies. There isn't always a lot of room for theology on the practical level, and it is easy to create a program that leaves theology at the door. What is called for is a practical or praxis theology—theology in action. Our Care of

Creation staff work hard to integrate theology throughout our projects: "Farming God's Way", "Planting God's Trees", "Harvesting God's Water" are more than slogans. We use them to remind participants and staff alike that everything we do is related to God and His original creative designs for this earth.

I believe an emphasis on sound theology will encourage a central role for the church in every country. "Mobilizing the church" means just that, whether the church in question is in Boston or Nairobi, Boise or Manila. Modern missiology recognizes that planting churches means accepting those churches as full partners in the work of the Kingdom. We will want to be sure that our model for creation care missions places the responsibility for God's creation where it belongs—on the shoulders of each local church body. The church in Kenya will answer to God for the condition of His creation in her corner of the world. We Christians in Madison, Wisconsin, will answer for what we have done to ours. We can and should help each other, but this shared responsibility is an acknowledgement that in each place the church is key to responding to the environmental crisis. A theologically sound program will focus on empowering and equipping the church to respond to whatever environmental challenges are evident in its particular area.

What does 'sound theology' mean in practice?

- *It means creating strategies and plans that are Biblically based.* It is easy to leave the theology at the door—this is something we have to resist. The power of the church comes from our beliefs and our reliance on God day by day. It can't be lip service.

- *It means working through local church structures.* In every setting, the church that God has placed there is the party whom God has entrusted with the care of his creation. All of our projects and efforts have to be designed to strengthen and help this local church to be what God wants it to be.

- *It means developing staff teams that know why they are doing what they are doing, and that are constantly being reminded of the underlying theological principles.* Training in technical subjects should

be paired with appropriate Biblical teaching, both on the job
and in regular refresher training courses.

- *It means relying on prayer as much as planning.* Sometimes you
  just have to go out and clean a stream bed. But there are times
  when both private and group prayer before, during and after a
  project will make the stream bed project go more smoothly and
  seem more pleasant.

## Good science

Good theology is vitally important, but theologians are probably not the best people to tell us what kind of trees to plant.
We have to be careful that our efforts are *scientifically informed.*
God has given us a complex world, and mistakes are easy to
make and hard to fix. Take the eucalyptus tree. Fast growing,
adaptable, commercially valuable wood—it seemed like the answer to Kenya's deforestation problem. Hundreds of square
miles of eucalyptus were planted. Another success, yes? Not
so fast. It turns out that this tree, designed by God for its native
Australia, wasn't quite as ideal for Africa as it first appeared.
For one thing, the eucalyptus is a thirsty tree. In a dry climate,
where every drop of water counts, a grove of eucalyptus acts
like a giant pump, sucking water out of the soil and away from
all of the trees and plants around it. An African sister told me
recently, "If your neighbor has a Eucalyptus tree, forget it. Your
own farm will be dry." Then it turned out that African insects
didn't like eucalyptus. The fragrant oils that Australian animals like the koala love drive African bugs away. While this
would not seem to be a problem to me and to you, it's a big
problem for birds that eat bugs. With no native insects, African
birds can't live in eucalyptus groves either. A God–designed
ecosystem has plants, animals, birds and insects that know each
other, need each other and live well together. A system that
tries to combine Australian trees and African bugs and birds
just doesn't work. As eucalyptus spreads, habitat for birds de-
creases and water problems increase.

Some mistakes are reversible, and this is one. A number of years ago, Brackenhurst International Conference Center, where our Kenya project is based, began removing eucalyptus trees and replacing them with indigenous African varieties. Almost immediately the birdwatchers in the area noticed a difference. Before the project began, a survey found 30 species of local birds on the grounds. This number is tragically low for Kenya, which claims to have more native bird species than any other single country, with a count of 1089 native bird species. Recently, just a few years after the eucalyptus were replaced with bird-friendly African trees, a visiting couple was able to count 140 species.

Here are a few suggestions to be sure that a missions project is scientifically sound:

- *Use people with appropriate environmental or scientific backgrounds throughout the project process.* Scientifically qualified advice need not be expensive. One of the virtues of scientists is that they are often looking for places to test their ideas, and (sometimes) they have money or can write grants on their own. I know of several college professors who have spent a number of years traveling to various parts of the world to share their expertise. This is a benefit for those of us working in those countries, but also benefits the professors who are able to bring real-world experience back to their students. Hosting a professor for a semester or year long sabbatical is a way to gain top level advice at very little cost. You may find that you have access to international NGOs or intergovernmental organizations like the United Nations Environmental Program (UNEP) in your area who would be pleased to partner with you. Your "successful" project makes them look good, too.

- *Establish a planning-implementing-review cycle that allows you to know what is really going on in your project area.* This means allowing enough time at the front end to ensure that you really understand the needs of the area; going in without predetermined ideas as to what the project is going to be about; ruthlessly evaluating every aspect of a project to see if the short and long term goals you wanted to achieve were actually met. The planning process is key, but review is an equally important phase that we often overlook in the mission world.

- *Avoid "donor-driven" project goals.* Donors or board members may have pet project ideas that are not what is needed in a given situation. During the Pakistan earthquake recovery my staff and I came across a "straw bale house" being constructed by a major international relief organization. Straw bale construction is an innovative construction technique that is very appropriate in some parts of the world—but not in northern Pakistan. We were intrigued, and stopped to ask what the background to this project was. It turned out the organization had a wealthy donor who was convinced that straw bale is the answer to everything, and so they were building a straw bale house to please him. This happens more often than we want to admit. The customer may always be right in retail, but the donor is not always right. Approach your donor with solid technical and scientific reasons for your proposed project; reputable donor agencies will appreciate your work ahead of time, and so will the project participants.

- *Develop student internship or research sponsoring programs.* Like professorial sabbaticals, these are opportunities to benefit from the presence of a person who has been studying the latest material, while giving them the chance to apply and test that material. Internships are normally taken by students in the upper levels of undergraduate work or between undergrad and graduate programs. Research would be conducted by Masters or Ph.D. candidate students.

## Geographical awareness

Finally, a mission strategy should be *geographically comprehensive.* Until now, many mission efforts, including environmental projects, have been local in focus and scale. One village or one neighborhood or perhaps a group of villages are targeted for evangelism or relief efforts. Some projects, like tree planting or watershed restoration work effectively at this level, since local people are affected by the problems and can be involved in remediation efforts. Environmental problems often do not respect community boundaries or national borders and geographically comprehensive strategies are needed.

For example, consider a current set of problems in Kenya. In overcrowded slums in a city like Nairobi, people have to have fuel to cook their food. They buy charcoal from street vendors—there is no other fuel available. Their demand for charcoal drives deforestation deep in the hills miles from the city, as equally poor people sneak into national forest reserves, sometimes bribing government officials who often aren't rich either, to cut down trees and burn them into charcoal. These activities in turn devastate farmland miles away and far down the slopes from the forest where the trees were actually removed. Without the forest, the farmers' water source becomes erratic, swinging from drought to flood and back again. The farmer himself is also collecting wood for his own use or for charcoal.

Part of Care of Creation's work is to help this farmer to manage his land carefully and in accordance with biblical and scientific principles. We have found that farmers are eager to learn and will want to do everything they can to preserve remaining land. But as long as the trees continue to be cut on the slopes above his small farm, the farmer is fighting a losing battle. The government officials who manage the forest, and who also are probably Christians, need to care for the forest with a new sincerity. Even then, they will be unable to stem the tide unless some alternative fuel source is provided for the residents of the Nairobi slum.

How can we create projects that address needs comprehensively rather than piecemeal?

- *Do your scientific homework first.* Good preliminary research and surveys should uncover the links between local problems and problems in other areas.

- *Establish regional partnerships with other organizations and regional government offices.* If organization A is doing reforestation upstream and organization B is working on erosion control for farmers downstream in the same watershed, a great deal synergy can result from regular consultations and active partnerships. In the case of Care of Creation's work in Kenya, we are seeking to encourage churches and schools over a wide area to establish nurseries and to develop their own tree-planting programs. Some of those churches are in areas where other development organizations are at work, and it is helpful for both them and us when we can let each other know what we are doing.

• *In keeping with the theological principle of strengthening the local church, encourage churches and denominations to establish their own regional or national partnerships.* Care of Creation's biannual God and Creation conferences have begun to create such networks in the Christian community in Kenya. We would like to see such conferences held in the neighboring countries as well, and eventually throughout the African continent and beyond. Blending Bible teaching with practical workshops, such conferences result in effective training, increased enthusiasm and a healthy network of relationships between churches and the people in those churches across the conference area.

Problems like these cannot be solved without becoming involved in political and economic realities. Aggressive and affirmative government action is sometimes the only way forward. While this is not the role of a mission organization, it is the legitimate role of the church in each country. How could this happen? Church members, ordinary Christians whom God has placed in positions of critical influence, can create and enforce policies to preserve God's creation. They will understand— because of teaching from their pastors and because of their own convictions—that this is what Christians do. Others will enforce the rules they have been sent to enforce as government officials for the same reason—their faith tells them to be faithful in this task. Farmers and city dwellers alike will make small, daily decisions to live simply and to walk the earth softly because they have been taught that this is the same earth Jesus walked on, and that the redemption that means so much in their own lives also has meaning for the birds, animals and trees.

This is how a mobilized church can change the world.

# twelve

## AND FINALLY ...

On October 8, 2005, a devastating earthquake shook the northern mountains of Pakistan. 76,000 people died. Thousands more sustained serious injury. Hundreds of thousands of homes were destroyed. Around the world, millions of people watched, listened, and responded to the crisis. I arrived in Islamabad at 7 AM on November 8 one month after the quake. By 8 AM I found myself sitting at an enormous conference table with forty or fifty people who represented some of the many organizations engaged in the massive relief effort. Some represented government or large nonprofit organizations and were clearly professional 'disaster fighters'. Others, like me, had been called in from other duties and occupations for a month or longer to do what needed to be done. The sense of urgency was evident. Winter was coming, and the possibility was real that initial disaster could be compounded by thousands more deaths from five to ten feet of snow that could be expected.

The effort to beat the winter emergency was called Project Winter Race. And it succeeded. Tents, emergency shelters, blankets, stoves and food were distributed in huge numbers. Many strategies were tried, and organizations quickly adapted to focus on the most successful approaches. Convoys of trucks

and jeeps and an international fleet of helicopters ferried supplies to the most remote locations. One United Nations official
called this one of the most complicated but best run disaster
recovery operations he had ever seen.

There were hundreds of organizations involved, but the organizations were not the heroes. The heroes of the Pakistan
earthquake were ordinary people who made extraordinary efforts. A doctor in Sweden came and served beside another
from Korea. A group of eighty Cuban doctors who could speak
neither English nor Urdu but who communicated a love and
compassion for people drew praise from all sides. Construction workers from California heard that help was needed building emergency shelters, gave up vacation time, and paid for
their own tickets. And many ordinary Pakistanis gave time and
money to help their countrymen during a time of need.

When disasters occur, it is people who make the difference.
Organizations are just tools. They help us coordinate and work
together, but their effectiveness (or lack thereof) is in the individuals who sit behind the desks, answer the phones or drive
the trucks. In this book we've been talking about *mobilizing the
church to respond to the environmental crisis.* But in the end, *the
church* can't respond. Only individual Christians like you and
me can do that. We should work in and through our church
families to involve others and to multiply our efforts. But my
church and yours will remain on the sidelines *until some one in
that church decides to do something.* Some of us could legitimately
say that we are 'just ordinary folks', others have positions of
considerable influence and responsibilities for leadership. But
all of us have a personal responsibility to do what we can where
ever we are right now.

May I address my final words to some specific people in the
Church?

*Dear Pastor,*

In the Prologue I referred to *The Creation,* formulated as a letter to a pastor. Professor Wilson recognized two things: Religion—the church—is influential in society, and pastors are influential within the church. Those of us who are or have been pastors may chuckle at that—we know how little influence we really have at times. But I'm not sure that Wilson is entirely wrong, though he might not understand why or how he is right. What I am thinking of is the unique power of preaching. The preaching of the Word remains a sacramental act—it is not the same as a lecture at the university, and packs more punch than a movie distributed nationwide. It is an awesome and sacred duty, and carries potential for influence far greater than many of us who practice it realize. When the Word of God is delivered to the people of God by an authentic servant of God, the Spirit of God can do His work in the lives of those people.

So I am asking you, Pastor, to consider, as you wield this powerful weapon of the Spirit every week, whether and to what extent you are using it to bring your people a full understanding of God's redemptive plan as it relates to all of creation. This kind of preaching takes sincerity, spiritual authenticity, and courage. It may require you to challenge some of the preconceived opinions of those in your congregation. Tri Robinson, author of *Saving God's Green Earth,* waited years before he preached to his people about caring for God's creation, though he knew God was calling him to do it. He admits that he was afraid of what the reaction would be. To his amazement, the reaction was a standing ovation. His fears were groundless. He need not have waited so long. But what if it had been otherwise? Fear is not an acceptable reason for neglecting to preach the full word of God.

There are some disturbing parallels between the stand the church is willing to take now on environmental issues and the way previous generations of evangelicals wavered on the im-

portant questions of slavery and civil rights. It is obvious now
that those pastors and churches who remained silent or who
even actively opposed those issues were wrong. Embarrass-
ingly wrong. Even tragically wrong. Let's not make the same
mistake again.

On this point Wilson is right: As a pastor, you have a key
role in the response to this crisis. May God give you grace—and
courage—to play your part.

*Dear Church Member,*

You don't think you're anyone special. Just an ordinary Joe
or Jane who sits half way back in the sanctuary on the left hand
side. You love your Bible, though you may never have opened
a book on theology in your life. Your Christian life consists
of being faithful in the little things. You pray for friends and
relatives who are lost. You grieve when you hear about hungry
people and orphans in other countries. You worry about your
kids and grandkids and what kind of world is going to be left
for them. But the problems seem too big. What can you do?

I want to encourage you to begin to make changes where
you can. Little things make a big difference. Did you know, for
example, that water consumption in the US has not increased
for almost 20 years, even though our population has increased
dramatically in that time? Do you want to know how? You
were part of it: Water-saving shower heads and low-flow toilets
were mandated in many parts of the country in the late 1970s
and 1980s. It doesn't seem like much, but the 10 or 20 gallons
saved on each shower multiplied by 300 million people is a lot
of water. We saved enough collectively to accommodate millions of more people with enough to go around—and few of us
even noticed. We need to do this in other areas. And we can do
this. We don't have to wait for someone to tell us to reduce our
electricity consumption by 10 % (and that's easy). Similarly, we
can start reducing our driving. We can learn to purchase and
consume less and use products that do less damage when we

do use them. We can learn to walk lightly on this earth. Pick up my friend Matthew Sleeth's book, *Serve God, Save the Planet*— it's loaded with advice.

I also want to encourage you to speak up in your local church. Sometimes one voice that speaks up at just the right time can make all the difference. I remember being at a basketball game in my freshman year in college. Getting a bit overly enthusiastic, I shouted something not very complimentary about the referee at the exact moment when there was one of those random silences in the crowd. My voice rang out, much louder and clearer than I intended, resulting in a good deal of embarrassment on my part. You don't know how effective your one voice might be when you speak up so do so. Let people know that you would like to use something besides disposable dishes at church dinners. Encourage your pastor or Sunday school leaders to teach creation care. See if your missions program is involved in any kind of overseas creation care projects. Ask your office manager to buy recycled paper for the copier. Express your convictions about these things and you will find other people who feel the same way you do. Did you know that 40 % of the members of the Sierra Club are people of faith who attend worship services regularly? Tragically, they hide their church membership while at Sierra Club meetings, and their Sierra membership while at church. The result? Neither the Sierra Club nor the church reflects their views. You might be one of these. Speak up at both places, and discover how many friends you have.

### Dear Student,

You have been on my mind all the way through this book. I was your age—or a bit younger, perhaps— when I was first touched by the environmental crisis on that first Earth Day, 1970. Many years slipped by before I picked up the topic again, or rather, before it found me. I'm afraid you don't have that luxury. The crisis is upon us. Time is running out. But even humanly speaking, we are not without hope, at least not yet. If we can take the appropriate steps now, and manage our collective global affairs carefully for the next 50 or 75 years until the human population stabilizes, we can navigate what Professor Wilson calls the bottleneck: We can arrive at a place where human population is stable, and the nonhuman portion of creation is still intact and functioning. But we have to begin now.

As Interstate 90 enters downtown Cleveland from the east, it runs along the shore of Lake Erie, and then makes a sharp—and I do mean sharp—left hand turn to head south into the center of the city. On a highway where the speed limit is 55 miles per hour, and most traffic goes 65 or better, a turn that can only be navigated at about 30 miles per hour is a major hazard. Traffic engineers know this, and so for a good two miles before that turn, they have installed some of the largest warning signs and flashing lights I have seen on the Interstate system. The reason for all the warning signs is simple: If drivers slow down in time, they can manage the turn without difficulty or danger. If there were no warning signs, and they had to wait until they could see the turn to slow down, for many it would be too late to avoid a crash. The environmental trends we are seeing in the paper every day are like those warning signs and the message is the same: SLOW DOWN NOW!

The global civilization is racing toward such a turn now. As a student now, you will be at the height of your career when we hit the corner. The career decisions you make now will allow you to be among those who are stepping on the brake rather than the accelerator. In the first chapter, you will recall, we concluded that the world is crying for leaders—people who will step up with knowledge (training), imagination, and courage to guide our collective response to the environmental crisis. I challenge you to be one of those leaders.

Our situation is as urgent as the Winter Race effort after the Pakistan earthquake, though it will play out over your entire career rather than the next six or seven weeks. What should you be considering? There are a host of fields in which you can have an impact: Scientists are needed who can work in the desperately shorthanded fields of botanical and zoological taxonomy. We have to name many creatures so we know how to save them. (Talk about a divine mission: Naming the creatures was one of Adam's first jobs.) We will need political leaders and policy makers who will guide communities and nations in preserving God's creation; business people who will lead the way in developing an economy that can feed and clothe the human race without destroying itself. And we need pastors and church leaders who will make caring for God's creation the priority it must be. Especially the latter: The church must be mobilized if all the rest is to happen.

We don't choose the times in which we are born, or the tasks that are presented to us. I could wish that my own generation had made some different decisions along the way that would have made your task easier. Regretfully, we didn't. But we can still move forward together.

We could do worse than to remember Elrond's words in J.R.R. Tolkien's Fellowship of the Ring as he addressed the Council just before Frodo agreed to carry the Ring to Mordor:

> *The road must be trod, but it will be very hard. And neither strength nor wisdom will carry us far upon it. This quest may be attempted by the weak with as much hope as the strong. Yet such is oft the course of deeds that move the wheels of the world: small hands do them because they must, while the eyes of the great are elsewhere.*
> [Tolkien, *Fellowship of the Ring*, 283]

# Appendix I

# Mobilizing God's People

## A Declaration for Action by Delegates of the 2nd International Conference on God & Creation

*The following declaration was signed by more than 200 church leaders from Kenya and twenty other countries on March 11, 2006, at Care of Creation's conference at Brackenhurst International Conference Center, Tigoni, Kenya. (See Chapter 5.)*

**As leaders and members of the evangelical church body in East Africa, representing a wide range of denominations and ministries, we stand together in agreement with the following declaration:**

We believe in one God, the Creator, Owner, and Sustainer of all things, and we uphold the truth that His creation serves as a dynamic testimony of His power, wisdom, and glory.

As followers of Christ, we believe that God calls us to be good stewards of His creation. We embrace the truth that caring for creation brings glory to God, and that it serves as a practical expression of our love and concern for both current and future generations.

Upon reflection at this conference, we believe the environmental crisis emerging in East Africa poses a critical threat to our future. The creation is suffering as a result of deforestation, the degradation of agricultural and pastoral lands, pollution, the loss of biodiversity, and the greed of man. This is undermining the well-being of our communities and is leading to the impoverishment of our people.

We confess that the church has responded poorly to this issue. Our failure in promoting and exercising proper stewardship over the creation has undermined our witness for Christ, and we hereby declare that we repent of our sin and negligence in this matter.

Acknowledging that the Author of our salvation is also the Author of all creation (Jn 1:1-3 and Col 1:16), we also declare that, more than any other group of people, it is believers committed to sharing the love and truth of Christ who should take the lead in responding to this crisis. We believe that awakening the church to action is our most promising hope in the spiritual and physical battle against environmental degradation in the 21st century.

We therefore appeal to all church and denominational leaders to recognize the gravity of the situation and to begin developing God-centered strategies to educate, disciple, and mobilize the entire church to action. Our prayer is that God will initiate a powerful movement which will sweep across Africa and have an impact worldwide.

As we join together in a spirit of humility and repentance, and begin taking the necessary action, we have reason for great hope! According to II Chronicles 7:14 this is the essential first step we must take if God is to bring healing to our land.

> *If my people, who are called by my name, will humble themselves and pray and seek my face and turn from their wicked ways, then I will hear from heaven and will forgive their sin and will heal their land.*

# Appendix II

# An Evangelical Declaration on the Care of Creation

*Signed in 1994 by almost 300 Evangelical leaders, this historic document is the fruit of discussions begun at an Au Sable Institute Forum in August 1992 that led to a substantial report, Evangelical Christianity and the Environment and eventually to the formation of the Evangelical Environmental Network (EEN), now ably led by the Rev. James Ball. The story of the writing of this declaration, and extensive commentary on the issues and theology behind it, can be found in R.J. Berry, (editor), The Care of Creation (2000).*

*We have reprinted the document here because it is a significant evangelical statement on the issues addressed in this book, and ought not to be lost, even in the dust of recent history, but also because it represents a good starting point for any church or evangelical organization seeking a concise theological platform from which to begin formulating their own response to creation care issues. The full list of signatories can be found on the EEN website* (http://www.creationcare.org/resources/signatores.php).

## *"The Earth is the Lord's and the fullness thereof"*

As followers of Jesus Christ, committed to the full authority of the Scriptures, and aware of the ways we have degraded creation, we believe that biblical faith is essential to the solution of our ecological problems.

**Because** we worship and honor the Creator, we seek to cherish and care for the creation.

**Because** we have sinned, we have failed in our stewardship of creation. Therefore we repent of the way we have polluted, distorted, or destroyed so much of the Creator's work.

**Because** in Christ God has healed our alienation from God and extended to us the first fruits of the reconciliation of all things, we commit ourselves to working in the power of the Holy Spirit to share the Good News of Christ in word and deed, to work for the reconciliation of all people in Christ, and to extend Christ's healing to suffering creation.

**Because** we await the time when even the groaning creation will be restored to wholeness, we commit ourselves to work vigorously to protect and heal that creation for the honor and glory of the Creator— whom we know dimly through creation, but meet fully through Scripture and in Christ. We and our children face a growing crisis in the health of the creation in which we are embedded, and through which, by God's grace, we are sustained. Yet we continue to degrade that creation.

**These** degradations of creation can be summed up as 1) land degradation; 2) deforestation; 3) species extinction; 4) water degradation; 5) global toxification; 6) the alteration of atmosphere; 7) human and cultural degradation.

**Many** of these degradations are signs that we are pressing against the finite limits God has set for creation. With continued population growth, these degradations will become more severe. Our responsibility is not only to bear and nurture children, but to nurture their home on earth. We respect the institution of marriage as the way God has given to insure thoughtful procreation of children and their nurture to the glory of God.

**We** recognize that human poverty is both a cause and a consequence of environmental degradation. Many concerned people, convinced that environmental problems are more spiritual than technological, are exploring the world's ideologies and religions in search of non-Christian spiritual resources for the healing of the earth. As followers of Jesus Christ, we believe that the Bible calls us to respond in four ways:

**First**, God calls us to confess and repent of attitudes which devalue creation, and which twist or ignore biblical revelation to support our misuse of it. Forgetting that "the earth is the Lord's," we have often simply used creation and forgotten our responsibility to care for it.

**Second,** our actions and attitudes toward the earth need to proceed from the center of our faith, and be rooted in the fullness of God's revelation in Christ and the Scriptures. We resist both ideologies which would presume the Gospel has nothing to do with the care of non-human creation and also ideologies which would reduce the Gospel to nothing more than the care of that creation.

**Third,** we seek carefully to learn all that the Bible tells us about the Creator, creation, and the human task. In our life and words we declare that full good news for all creation which is still waiting "with eager longing for the revealing of the children of God," (Rom. 8:19).

**Fourth,** we seek to understand what creation reveals about God's divinity, sustaining presence, and everlasting power, and what creation teaches us of its God-given order and the principles by which it works.

Thus we call on all those who are committed to the truth of the Gospel of Jesus Christ to affirm the following principles of biblical faith, and to seek ways of living out these principles in our personal lives, our churches, and society.

**The cosmos,** in all its beauty, wildness, and life-giving bounty, is the work of our personal and loving Creator.

**Our creating God** is prior to and other than creation, yet intimately involved with it, upholding each thing in its freedom, and all things in relationships of intricate complexity. God is transcendent, while lovingly sustaining each creature; and immanent, while wholly other than creation and not to be confused with it.

**God the Creator** is relational in very nature, revealed as three persons in One. Likewise, the creation which God intended is a symphony of individual creatures in harmonious relationship.

**The Creator's concern** is for all creatures. God declares all creation "good" (Gen. 1:31); promises care in a covenant with all creatures (Gen. 9:9-17); delights in creatures which have no human apparent usefulness (Job 39-41); and wills, in Christ, "to reconcile all things to himself" (Col.1:20).

**Men, women, and children**, have a unique responsibility to the Creator; at the same time we are creatures, shaped by the same processes and embedded in the same systems of physical, chemical, and biological interconnections which sustain other creatures.

**Men, women, and children**, created in God's image, also have a unique responsibility for creation. Our actions should both sustain creation's fruitfulness and preserve creation's powerful testimony to its Creator.

**Our God-given, stewardly talents** have often been warped from their intended purpose: that we know, name, keep and delight in God's creatures; that we nourish civilization in love, creativity and obedience to God; and that we offer creation and civilization back in praise to the Creator. We have ignored our creaturely limits and have used the earth with greed, rather than care.

**The earthly result** of human sin has been a perverted stewardship, a patchwork of garden and wasteland in which the waste is increasing. "There is no faithfulness, no love, no acknowledgment of God in the land ... Because of this the land mourns, and all who live in it waste away" (Hosea 4:1,3). Thus, one consequence of our misuse of the earth is an unjust denial of God's created bounty to other human beings, both now and in the future.

**God's purpose in Christ** is to heal and bring to wholeness not only persons but the entire created order. "For God was pleased to have all his fullness dwell in him, and through him to reconcile to himself all things, whether things on earth or things in heaven, by making peace through his blood shed on the cross" (Col. 1:19-20).

**In Jesus Christ**, believers are forgiven, transformed and brought into God's kingdom. "If anyone is in Christ, there is a new creation" (II Cor. 5:17). The presence of the kingdom of God is marked not only by renewed fellowship with God, but also by renewed harmony and justice between people, and by renewed harmony and justice between people and the rest of the created world. "You will go out in joy and be led forth in peace; the mountains and the hills will burst into song before you, and all the trees of the field will clap their hands" (Isa. 55:12).

**We believe** that in Christ there is hope, not only for men, women and children, but also for the rest of creation which is suffering from the consequences of human sin. Therefore we call upon all Christians to reaffirm that all creation is God's; that God created it good; and that God is renewing it in Christ.

**We encourage deeper reflection** on the substantial biblical and theological teaching which speaks of God's work of redemption in terms of the renewal and completion of God's purpose in creation.

**We seek a deeper reflection** on the wonders of God's creation and the principles by which creation works. We also urge a careful consideration of how our corporate and individual actions respect and comply with God's ordinances for creation.

**We encourage Christians** to incorporate the extravagant creativity of God into their lives by increasing the nurturing role of beauty and the arts in their personal, ecclesiastical, and social patterns.

**We urge individual Christians** and churches to be centers of creation's care and renewal, both delighting in creation as God's gift, and enjoying it as God's provision, in ways which sustain and heal the damaged fabric of the creation which God has entrusted to us.

**We recall Jesus' words** that our lives do not consist in the abundance of our possessions, and therefore we urge followers of Jesus to resist the allure of wastefulness and overconsumption by making personal lifestyle choices that express humility, forbearance, self restraint and frugality.

**We call on all Christians** to work for godly, just, and sustainable economies which reflect God's sovereign economy and enable men, women and children to flourish along with all the diversity of creation. We recognize that poverty forces people to degrade creation in order to survive; therefore we support the development of just, free economies which empower the poor and create abundance without diminishing creation's bounty.

**We commit ourselves** to work for responsible public policies which embody the principles of biblical stewardship of creation.

**We invite Christians**—individuals, congregations and organizations—to join with us in this evangelical declaration on the environment, becoming a covenant people in an ever-widening circle of biblical care for creation.

**We call upon Christians** to listen to and work with all those who are concerned about the healing of creation, with an eagerness both to learn from them and also to share with them our conviction that the God whom all people sense in creation (Acts 17:27) is known fully only in the Word made flesh in Christ the living God who made and sustains all things.

**We make this declaration** knowing that until Christ returns to reconcile all things, we are called to be faithful stewards of God's good garden, our earthly home.

# Appendix III
# About Care of Creation, Inc.

Care of Creation, Inc., is a Christian environmental organization, seeking to awaken and mobilize the Church to care for God's creation in the face of an environmental crisis that is already devastating vast areas of the world.

We are also a missions organization. We believe that environmental problems are sin problems, and we are convinced that the Church of Jesus Christ is the world's best hope for dealing with this crisis.

We believe that missions and care for God's creation belong together.

We're about...

- Loving God by worshiping him in all we do;
- Loving God's People by sharing the good news we have in Jesus Christ, and by strengthening and empowering local Congregations to join in...
- Loving God's World by working with and through his people to care for and heal God's hurting creation.

We are at work...

- In Kenya through *Care of Creation—Kenya* based at the well-known Brackenhurst Conference Center in Limuru;
- In the United States through services and consultation through our Madison, WI. home office.

We invite you...

- To partner with us by supporting our work with your prayers and your gifts; Care of Creation is a 501(c)(3) organization  all gifts are tax deductible. Donate through our website or by mail using the contact information below.

- To contact us for more information and who we are and what we do

**Care of Creation Inc.**
**PO Box 44582**
**Madison, WI 53744**
**www.careofcreation.org**

# For further reading

Berry, R.J., ed., *The Care of Creation: Focusing Concern and Action*. Leicester, England: InterVarsity Press, 2000.

Berry, Wendell , *The Art of the Commonplace: The Agrarian Essays of Wendell Berry*. Emeryville, California: Shoemaker Hoard, 2002.

Bouma-Prediger, Steven, *For the Beauty of the Earth: A Christian Vision for Creation Care*. Grand Rapids, Michigan: Baker Book House, 2001.

Bouma-Prediger, Steven, *The Greening of Theology: The Ecological Models of Rosemary Radford Ruether, Joseph Sittler, and Jurgen Moltmann*. Atlanta, Georgia: American Academy of Religion, 1995.

Brown, Lester R., *Plan B 2.0: Rescuing a Planet Under Stress and a Civilisation in Trouble*. New York: W.W. Norton, 2006.

Bryson, Bill., *A Short History of Nearly Everything*. New York: Broadway Books , 2003.

Collins, Francis , *The Language of God: A Scientist Presents Evidence for Belief*. New York: Simon Schuster, 2006.

DeWitt, Calvin, *Earth-Wise: A Biblical Response to Environmental Issues*. Grand Rapids, Michigan: CRC Publications, 1994.

DeWitt, Calvin, ed. , *The Just Stewardship of Land and Creation: A Report of the Reformed Ecumenical Council*. Grand Rapids, Michigan: Reformed Ecumenical Council, 1996.

Diamond, Jared , *Collapse: How Societies Choose to Succeed or Fail*. New York: Penguin, 2005.

Fortey, Richard, *The Earth: An Intimate History*. London: HarperCollins, 2004.

Friedman, Thomas L. , *The World Is Flat*. New York: Farrar, Straus and Giroux, 2006.

Hall, Douglas John, *Imaging God: Dominion as Stewardship*. Grand Rapids, Michigan: Wm B. Eerdmans, 1986.

Hoezee, Scott , *Remember Creation: God's World of Wonder and Delight*. Grand Rapids: Wm B. Eerdmans, 1998.

Jones, James , *Jesus and the Earth*. London: SPCK Publishing, 2005.

McDonough, William and Braungart, Michael , *Cradle to Cradle: Remaking the Way We Make Things*. New York: North Point Press, 2002.

Robinson, Tri, *Saving God's Green Earth: Rediscovering the Church's responsibility to environmental stewardship*. Norcross, Georgia: Ampelon, 2006.

Rodin, R. Scott , *Stewards in the Kingdom: A Theology of Life in All Its Fullness*. Downers Grove, Illinois: InterVarsity Press, 2000.

Schaeffer, Francis A., *Pollution and the Death of Man*. Wheaton, Illinois: Tyndale House, 1970.

Schweiger, Larry. "A Call to Evangelicals to Join the Debate", *Creation Care Magazine*. : , 2005.

Sleeth, J. Matthew, *Serve God, Save the Planet: A Christian Call to Action*. White River Junction, Vermont: Chelsea Green , 2006.

Seuss, *The Lorax*, 1971.

Walton, John. "Genesis", *The NIV Application Commentary*, Terry Muck, ed. Grand Rapids: Zondervan, 2001.

White, Lynn. *Science* **155**, 1203 (1967).

Wilson, E.O., *The Future of Life*. New York: Knopf , 2002.

Wilson, E.O., *The Creation: An Appeal to Save Life on Earth*. New York: W.W. Norton, 2006.

Winter, Ralph, "The Uncertain Future of Missions", *Mission Frontiers*, **10-12** (2006).

# Aknowledgments

This book has been a family project. My wife Susanna deserves much credit for her encouragement, patience and prodding during the writing process. More than anyone else, she worked through the initial drafts and to the extent that the final product is interesting and readable, she is the one to thank. My children have been quick with comments, some of them valuable. The book is that much better for their suggestions.

Much appreciation goes to my brothers, Dan and Tom, who are the driving force behind Doorlight Publications, and who worked together to edit, typeset and coordinate production—and did it in record time.

And finally, my thanks to those from whom I learned the importance of Christian environmental stewardship  The Au Sable Institute family first, and my Care of Creation family in more recent years.

Where this book is helpful and encouraging, these are the people to thank. Where it falls short, the responsibility is mine.

Edward Brown
Madison, Wisconsin
November, 2006